Endorsements for
Bullying Under Attack

"Wow. What a timely achievement—the only book about the problem of bullying entirely written by teenagers. I know their personal stories will move you, anger you, inspire you—even scare you. A great read for a great cause."

—R. L. Stine, author of the *Goosebumps* series

"Heart-felt and heart-wrenching stories, straight from the experiences of the bullied, the bystanders, and those who have bullied. Exceptional writing from all, and so worth the read."

—Ellen Hopkins, *The New York Times* bestselling young adult author

"Bullying comes in many forms: name calling, shutting out, character assassination, humiliation . . . even getting spit at. All of which happened to me. This important book takes on an issue all of us can relate to because it happened to so many of us. It's refreshing and at times heartbreaking to hear the experiences of these young people. Their voices remind us that bullying is still an issue for children of all ages, and their stories bring a fresh perspective to an old story. *Bullying Under Attack* is a unique wakeup call for parents, teachers, and bullies, victims, and bystanders to stop, listen, and think about the power of their words and actions."

—Vanessa Williams

"I was never a victim . . . never a bully . . . but bystander? Oh, yes. I was too often a bystander. Maybe I am, sometimes still. This meaningful book will kindle sparks of recognition in many of us, along with a reminder that we can change."

—Lois Lowry, author of *The Giver*

"It's great that Teen Ink has given a wide array of teenagers a chance to speak out on bullying!"

—Emily Bazelon, author of *Sticks and Stones*

"Can there be any truer YA literature than that created by young adults themselves? These stories and poems about bullying are wrenchingly beautiful in their honesty and sometimes remarkable in their insight. I have to believe that they will serve as a welcome salve for the wounds and loneliness of those who are bullied as well as wake-up call for the bullies who so often cannot comprehend the pain they inflict."

—Todd Strasser, author of *The Wave*

"People say that some books are mirrors and some are windows. That is to say, readers can find themselves reflected in the stories, or see out of their own narrow lives into a broader view. The stories in this collection will do this for you."

—Gregory Maguire, Author of *Out of Oz*,
the *Final Volume of the Wicked Years*

"Without detracting from what experts understand about bullying, there is no substitute for direct testimony by victims, victimizers, and bystanders. In this unique collection, young people describe their own experiences vividly and, in the process, reveal what they have learned about others and about themselves."

—Howard Gardner, professor of education at Harvard University,
author of *Frames of Mind: The Theory of Multiple Intelligences*

"*Bullying Under Attack*'s gripping firsthand accounts take you inside bullying from every vantage point. Writing with honesty, clarity, and heart, these brave young people illuminate a topic society prefers to squint at. Inspiring."

—Emma McLaughlin and Nicola Kraus,
authors of *The Nanny Diaries*

"With bullying on everyone's mind, this book offers great insight into the real-life stories of those most affected: the victim, the bystander, and the bully. A must-read for parents, educators, and teens who want to understand the severity of the bully crisis."

—Peter Buffett, environmentalist and philanthropist

"For almost a quarter of a century, Teen Ink has been encouraging young people to write and then has published those pieces. These heartfelt essays and poems explore the issues faced by teenagers today. I applaud their efforts because they not only help young people deal with their own lives but also encourage the budding authors of the next generation."

—Anita Silvey, creator of *Children's Book-a-Day Almanac*

BULLYING UNDER ATTACK

TRUE STORIES WRITTEN BY TEEN VICTIMS, BULLIES + BYSTANDERS

A TEEN INK BOOK

Edited by Stephanie H. Meyer, John Meyer,
Emily Sperber and Heather Alexander

HCI
TEENS™
The Life Issues Publisher

Health Communications, Inc.
Deerfield Beach, Florida

www.hcibooks.com

306830827
C

Library of Congress Cataloging-in-Publication Data

Teen Ink : bullying under attack : true stories written by teen victims, bullies &
bystanders / Stephanie H. Meyer, John Meyer, Emily Sperber, Heather Alexander.
    pages cm
  ISBN-13: 978-0-7573-1760-6 (Paperback)
  ISBN-10: 0-7573-1760-X (Paperback)
  ISBN-13: 978-0-7573-1761-3 (ePub)
    1. Adolescence—Literary collections.   2. Youths' writings, American.
    1. Bullies—Fiction.   2. Adolescence—Literary collections.   3. Youths' writings.
    I. Meyer, Stephanie H.   II. Meyer, John.   III. Sperber, Emily.   IV. Alexander,
Heather.   V. Title: Bullying under attack.
PZ5.T2947 2013
[Fic]—dc23
                                                                          2013020767

Publisher: Health Communications, Inc.
            3201 S.W. 15th Street
            Deerfield Beach, FL 33442-8190

Cover design by Sherri Baker Hamilton
Interior formatting by Dawn Von Strolley Grove

We dedicate this book to
Matthew and Tommy Hong, our precious grandsons,
in hopes that you and your generation
never have to experience the bullying
described in this book.

CONTENTS

FOREWORD

That October 7 will always be the day that divides my life. Before that day, my son Ryan was a sweet, gentle, lanky 13-year-old fumbling his way through early adolescence and trying to establish his place in the often confusing and difficult social world of middle school. After that day, my son would be gone forever, another tragic teen death by suicide.

Ryan's life included a typical array of "healthy" and "normal" teen activities . . . or so it seemed. My son loved connecting online with friends after school and throughout the summer. But during the summer of 2003, he spent significantly more time online, mainly instant messaging (IM). I was concerned and felt compelled to remind him of our family's Internet safety rules:

1. No texting with strangers.
2. No giving any personal information (name/
   address/phone number) to strangers.
3. No secret passwords.

The last rule was just in case of emergencies. I told my children that they had to use the password I gave them for all their online accounts. I promised I would not read personal messages or spy on them, but "God forbid you just disappear one day, I will want instant access to all of your activities online." Never in a million years did I imagine this rule would one day be the key to unlocking the mystery of why my son ended his life.

A few days after Ryan's funeral, I logged on to his AOL IM account. That was the one place he spent most of his time during the last few months, and I was seeking clues to explain his final action. It was in that safe world of semi-anonymity that several of his classmates told me of the bullying and cyberbullying Ryan experienced in the months leading up to his suicide.

Certainly, my son was not the first boy in history to be bullied. But when I discovered a folder filled with chat exchanges and then interviewed his classmates, I realized that technology had created a weapon far more effective and far-reaching than bullying when I was a kid. It's one thing to be humiliated in front of a few kids. But it must be a totally different experience, compared to a generation ago, to have these hurts and humiliation witnessed by a far larger, online adolescent audience.

I believe my son would have survived these incidents of bullying and humiliation if they had taken place before the advent of the Internet. My son was an early casualty to what is now commonly referred to as cyberbullying, and his death was an early warning to our society that we'd better pay closer attention to how our children use technology.

Sadly, since then, I have learned that Ryan's bullying was far from being unique or rare. This book contains many stories with a cyberbullying component, and it seems the practice is always evolving as technology evolves. This online world of adolescents is complex and puzzling for school administrators and law enforcement to navigate, and our laws have not kept pace with the developing technology. Part of my mission in honoring Ryan's memory has been to work to change the laws and punishments for bullying.

I am credited with spearheading the Vermont Bullying Prevention bill in memory of my son. But the credit really should be shared with the many brave students who came to a rare joint Vermont State Senate and House public hearing. One by one, they approached the microphone and courageously shared their bullying stories. These victims felt the adult world had let them down and often made it worse with poorly thought-out intervention approaches. The men and women of the Vermont State Senate and House Education Committees were brought to tears. Shortly after the hearing, they unanimously voted to send my bill to the floor for a vote. It passed in a landslide victory and was signed into law just seven months after my son's death. I will forever be indebted to those brave students who helped me move the legislators to act.

What were not shared during that hearing were stories from bullies' and bystanders' perspectives. Perhaps it was expecting too much for young people playing those parts to advocate for such a law, but I realized that the complete picture was not portrayed during that hearing. To properly address this problem, we need to hear from the bully and the bystander too. We need to understand why one would choose to inflict pain on a peer, and why the bystander would choose to simply be the audience to these awful acts. Too often attention is paid only to the victim. As a society, we seem to have a need to analyze what is wrong with the target for being victimized in the first place. Surely they must need to build stronger self-esteem! But if we are to address the problem effectively, we can't just focus on the bullied kids. To truly understand and stop the problem, we must get inside the heads of the bully and the bystander as well.

In the pages that follow, you will get a more complete picture of bullying today. This eye-opening book is filled with short, powerful stories from all three perspectives—the bully, the bullied, and the bystander. From firsthand experience visiting nearly a thousand schools around the country telling Ryan's story these past 10 years, I can attest that true stories told from the heart have the best chance of reaching a heart. My hope is that this collection of essays will inspire more students to share in classroom discussions and will educate adults in how best to navigate the fragility of adolescence.

—John Halligan, Ryan's dad
http://www.RyansStory.org

To read more about Ryan's story, see "90 Minutes" in Chapter 6.

PREFACE

Sekunjalo! This is one of my favorite words; it's Zulu and means "now is the time!" I learned it when I was a filmmaker in South Africa. It's from the era during the struggle to end apartheid.

Now is the time for this book. Now is the time for us to tell our stories, connect, and declare an end to the era that said bullying is a rite of passage.

I made the film *Bully* as a gift to my twelve-year-old self, the one with bruised arms who felt voiceless. "*Sekunjalo,*" I said, years later, when I set out to document the cruelty and exclusion millions of kids face daily. I wanted to give a gift to all those who have experienced being bullied, by providing a place, not the glossy one from *Mean Girls*, but a real undeniable place for those who were warned not to tell their stories.

And the stories and poems in *Bullying Under Attack* are also told by real kids conveying their actions and feelings that everyone can connect with.

I recently chatted with Katy Butler, an eighteen-year-old from Michigan who took her connection to my film *Bully* and decided to make a change—something anyone can do.

Katy: Just like Lee and so many other kids, I was bullied in middle school. After I told my best friend I had a crush on a girl, I found that my friend wasn't okay with it. She and other kids teased me and called me names. They pushed me into walls and knocked my books out of my hands. One day, a group of guys came up behind me at my locker, asking me why I even bothered to show my face at school, because no one wanted me there. I tried to walk away, but they slammed my hand in my locker, breaking my finger, and then ran off laughing.

Lee: I know exactly how you must have felt: hurt, helpless, and alone, but that didn't stop you from taking a stand.

Katy: When I listened to the stories in your film, I saw myself there. I know sharing stories is a key to begin the critical conversation about bullying. Having a book like this accessible to anyone is so important, especially since these are real stories that, as horribly sad and terrifying as they may be, will give people like me hope. By standing up and speaking out and sharing our stories, we are telling people we will not stand for this kind of treatment anymore and want change!

Lee: That's exactly right. *Sekunjalo*—it's the time for this book; a place where kids share their stories for others to read and then share with their friends. These kids are the ones who are going to make the difference. I've seen schools where bullying just isn't cool. Their communities have taken the initiative to change the climate of their school. And it's the students, the parents, and the teachers who have to make that happen. It all begins with just one person willing to speak out and let others know that we shouldn't stand for bullying.

Katy: That's so true. It takes not just those who are being bullied but also the bystanders and the bullies. This book offers a unique glimpse into the stories from the bullies and the bystanders along with those who have been bullied. That variety of viewpoints gives everyone the chance to find a story to connect with and hopefully inspire them to want to make a difference. Through sharing our stories and connecting with others, we can create the necessary space to have the conversations to change the climate of bullying around the country.

—Lee Hirsch, writer and director of the film *Bully*

Acknowledgments

First, we must thank all the teenagers, past and present, responsible for making this book possible. We must also give our heartfelt thanks to those who have done so much to make this Teen Ink book a reality, especially Nicholas Kristof, *New York Times* Pulitzer-winning columnist and book author, who helped invaluably with this project.

When we started publishing *Teen Ink* magazine in the late 1980s, we never imagined we would be working with so many talented and devoted people. Some have played an enormous role in the overall success of our nonprofit Young Authors Foundation (that helps fund all our projects). Others devote themselves tirelessly to our monthly magazine and website, which is the source for *Bullying Under Attack*.

We are most fortunate to have all of these people in our lives:

Our children: Our son and daughter, Robert Meyer and Alison Meyer Hong, as well as Alison's husband, Michael, and Robert's wife, Katherine, have been a never-ending source of support since our start. Their love, insight, encouragement, and wisdom have helped guide us every step of the way.

Our staff: We couldn't have done it without our tireless co-workers. They are a constant source of help with advice and assistance: First and foremost, Emily Sperber, one of the editors of this book, as well as editor of the monthly magazine; Cindy Spertner, who has taken on the role of assistant editor and coordinator of this project; Susan Tuozzolo, who is a constant support in our office; and Katie Olsen, who has never failed to help us with all things technical.

In addition, we must give a special thanks to Adam Halwitz, our longtime high-school intern who is now a college senior. Adam has taken on numerous tasks at Teen Ink over the years, and we have relied on him in many ways for our books, magazine, and website. His editing and research for this book has been invaluable, and Adam continues to contribute to our success. We are very fortunate to have him as part of our staff for all these years.

Our other faithful intern, Alex Cline, whose opinion is always valued; Miki Abelow, who helped cull through many of the bullying submissions; and our longtime volunteer, Barbara Field, who has been a constant support for so many years.

David Emerson and Robert Kavanaugh helped us for many years as our magazine, website, and now this important book, have required their expert web development, programming, and technical assistance. We simply could not have done it all without them.

Our board: Richard Freedberg, Dr. Lowell Fox, and John Kaufman. And our important sources of support: Barbara Wand, Mollie Dunn, Pamela Lubell, as well as many friends and relatives.

Our publishing family at Health Communications, Inc.: We once again thank all the folks at HCI who have published, promoted, and believed in all our projects for over a decade: Peter Vegso; Tonya Woodworth, our editor; Ian Briggs, her assistant; Kim Weiss; Kelly Maragni and her staff; and Larissa Hise Henoch and her staff for their continued design creativity.

Introduction

Bullying Under Attack had its beginnings in 2012 when the *New York Times* columnist Nicholas Kristof wrote about this critical problem and then held a national contest through the *New York Times* for teens to write about their bullying experiences. Teen Ink partnered with Kristof to review thousands of submissions for the contest, and some of these best stories are included in this book.

Teen Ink was excited to work on this project, since we are a magazine, website, and book series whose mission is to publish teenagers' writing about what matters most to them, allowing teens to share their views with peers and adults around the world. During our organization's 24-year history, our staff has received thousands of submissions from teens who were courageous enough to tell us their very personal stories about bullying.

After reading so many of these pieces, we wanted to compile an anthology of the best ones written by those who are dealing with these issues right now. Therefore, from the many personal and heart-wrenching stories published on our website, printed in our magazine, and received from the *New York Times* contest, we've chosen a hundred of the most compelling pieces of prose, poetry, and art that we believe will be an eye-opener for teens and adults alike. This book provides a compelling, informative, and often heartbreaking look into this nationwide epidemic.

We've gathered together the voices of those who have been affected by bullying directly or indirectly and have tried to select a range of work that covers multiple perspectives and experiences. We've included, for example, pieces that deal specifically with the growing awareness of self-harm (cutting, eating disorders) and suicide as a result of bullying.

Other authors discuss how technology has expanded the range for bullying, taking it out of school and following teens into their homes and personal lives. The submissions we've seen over the years reveal that bullying affects whole communities, so we believe that a three-part approach—hearing from victims, bystanders, and bullies—is the most representative way to help get everyone's story heard.

We hope these poignant stories will resonate with anyone who's suffered the pain of being bullied and let them know that they are not alone. We have given voice to the bystander, whose guilt is often heartbreaking, and the bully, who was often a victim before they morphed into their role of power, as well as the victim, whose story is so often heart wrenching.

We welcome feedback from teens and adults in reaction to these stories, and we hope this will be an important part of the ongoing, national dialogue about bullying. Details on how to reach us, or how to send your story if you are a teen who has been a victim, a bully, or a bystander are provided at the end of this book. We would like to hear from you.

Thanks again to all the teenagers whose stories have made this book possible. We applaud your honesty, courage, and willingness to share your experiences with the world.

Stephanie H. Meyer and John Meyer
Founders of Teen Ink *magazine &* TeenInk.com

Chapter One

SAVAGE YOUNG BEASTS

*"In three words I can sum up
everything I've learned about
Life: it goes on."*

—*Robert Frost*

Never Again

Elizabeth Ditty

February 14 of my senior year, I was bullied for the last time. That day, I hit my breaking point and felt that suicide was my only option. As I ran through the hallway, my head swam in depression. My hands were shaking as they reached for my cell phone. I couldn't even remember how to speed-dial Mom.

I was the girl who got called fat every single day. The girl who camouflaged her pain by laughing really hard and talking too loud, drowning out the demeaning comments. The girl fighting an internal battle to get up, get ready, and go to school every morning. Yes, I was that fat girl waddling to school, getting honked at by the popular kids, and even getting snowballs thrown at her butt in the winter. I was the girl who ate lunch alone on the bench in front of the cafeteria doors. The girl who had one friend, but lost even her when her boyfriend called me names too.

I had a simple, deadly, desperate plan to escape the social torment I'd been facing since the fifth grade: leave school, lie in the street on my stomach, and wait until a speeding car came along. Then it would all be over.

Never before had I come so close to acting on this fatal fantasy, but that day I was feeling adrenaline I never even knew existed in my body. Then, as I passed the counselor's office, out of nowhere, a voice spoke to me. It said, "You need to change your life. You are going through this so you can help other bullied children." I dashed straight into the counselor's office, in desperate need of help.

The counselor was busy, but after taking one look at me a secretary sprinted to get him. I was soon inside his office, heaving, hiccupping, and hysterical. I have never cried like that in my life. Tears streamed down my face as I hugged the trash can, afraid of vomiting out my feelings.

After my crisis, I refused to go to school. But wallowing in self-pity and depression at home wasn't helping, and I finally decided not to be a victim any longer. I forced myself to get out of bed and write a letter. A letter to my bully. Three pages in red ink.

© 2013 Sandy Honig

Upon returning to school, I went to a prearranged meeting in the dean's office and read the letter to my bully. Out loud to his face. For the first time in my life I stood up to my tormentor.

Dear _____,

Think back to ninth grade. Every day in study hall you would call me "fat ass" and "beached whale." One day I wore shorts; you looked at your friends and said, "That shouldn't be allowed." Those words left your mouth in just one second, but they entered my consciousness and still refuse to leave.

After your comments, I wanted to die. Do you know that I go to bed and cry every night? I have thoughts of killing myself. Sometimes I don't know how I've made it this far. When I hit rock bottom, though, I remind myself that if I ended my life, you would win. I'm not going to let you win. No matter what you do, I'll be here to prove a point. To show that you can't crush me.

Do you know that all the hell I've endured in school is my reason to go on living? I am going to go to college, become a counselor, and help other victims of bullies like you. I understand the pain they live with, and I want to help them survive it. When I want to die, I think about helping those in need, just as many kind souls have helped me to survive.

Do you know that I am okay with how I look? When I look in the mirror I see beauty. What I can't stand is my inner-self, and you're the one who trained me to feel this way. When I entered school, I instantly felt like a second-class person. I listened to your comments and didn't stand up for myself. I accepted all the pain you caused me and never took action—until now.

Are you aware of how I feel just being near you? I feel like I am not worth anything because you can't look into my eyes, past my weight, and see a normal girl. Sitting in class near you makes me anxious every day.

I am your equal. I am no less than you, and I never will be! You have no right to point out my "faults" and try to cut me down every day. Sadly, I have learned to expect and passively accept your comments. I live with them and believe them. They are and always will be etched into my heart and mind. You should really think about what you say before you say it, because some people are not as strong as I am, and they really might end up killing themselves.

What you did on February 14th is NOT okay. What gives you the right to touch my personal belongings? Who gives you the power to state who sits at what table? When you threw my purse and books onto the floor, it hurt me more than all of the demeaning comments over the years. It hurt me so much that I wanted to kill myself. Your actions told me just where I fit in here: that I am a piece of shit that belongs on the floor.

What's even worse is that I almost accepted what you did to me, just like I accepted the names you called me every day. I almost believed you were right, because you are a god in this school. Everyone respects you and looks up to you.

You have violated me with your words and actions, and you should know that what may seem to you like jokes are ruining my life and causing me to miss school.

I am through being your victim. I am done tolerating and accepting it. I am determined to enjoy the last few months of high school. From this day forward, you are going to treat me with the respect I deserve.

He cried. Seriously, my bully cried. Then he apologized sincerely. For the rest of high school, I, the former social reject, was never bullied again.

That was six months ago. Look at me now—I'm a new person. I've undergone a transformation. I am a college freshman—a psychology major with plans to become a school counselor. I gave my first public speech on school bullying and got a standing ovation, and I didn't even cry! Now I don't have to fake my smile. I stay up late, laughing and talking with my roommate, who is my new best friend. I walk into a crowded cafeteria and feel welcome at numerous tables. I'm not afraid to approach new faces. I'm the student who can't wait to get to class.

I'm finally happy not only on the outside but on the inside as well. I am new. I am the person who I want to be. Finally.

I treasure my life each and every day. I question why I once wanted to end my life. I realize just how lucky I am. So many people are being bullied every day and don't realize yet that they can make it through and have a happy life. They don't know that the torture will end.

I am blessed beyond belief. I've found joy. I've found my meaning, my calling: to become a counselor and help kids struggling with bullying. I have a passion and a purpose, and it becomes clearer each day. I'm so grateful I gave myself a second chance to live and to help other bullied children survive and rise up.

I am finally who I want to be.

Slip 'n Slide

Autumn Bornholdt

All I could think for weeks was, *How many people have seen the picture? How many have saved it to their desktops?*

My story begins on a muggy day in August. My friends and I set up a Slip 'n Slide in my neighbor's backyard. After my turn down the slide, I was pulled into a group photo with two friends. Later, the picture was posted on Facebook. On that carefree summer day, I never imagined one picture could cause so much pain.

A few weeks later, at a gathering after the first football game of the year, my friends and I were reliving summer memories. Not surprisingly, the Slip 'n Slide day came up.

One of my friends asked me, "You've seen the picture, right?"

I didn't understand the look on her face, but I knew what picture she was talking about, so I laughed and told her I had seen it.

"See, you guys? I told you she'd think it was funny!" another friend piped up.

Suddenly a queasy feeling surged in the pit of my stomach. Maybe I didn't know what they were talking about after all.

"Can I go on to Facebook quickly?" I asked a friend. I logged on and started clicking through pictures from that day. Finally, I found the one in question. Only then did I understand what the big deal was. Apparently, all the slipping and sliding had taken a toll on my swimsuit; it had definitely slipped out of place.

Heat rushed to my cheeks as I messaged the girl who originally uploaded the photo, asking her to remove it, which she did. But the damage had been done. The picture had been online for two weeks.

Before I knew it my eyes were overflowing with tears. I blindly rushed upstairs and locked myself in a bedroom. I called the only two people I knew who could make me feel better. They managed to calm me down a little, but I was still mortified. These girls who were supposed to be my friends had failed to tell me that I was exposed in the picture. Even worse, they had laughed about it behind my back. Unfortunately, that was only the start of a chain of awful events.

A few days later, a small misunderstanding happened between the girl I thought was my best friend and me. Later, when I logged on to Facebook, I found my wall filled with nasty comments from almost every one of our mutual friends. Even girls who had no knowledge of the details of the misunderstanding were taking part. Horrified, I clicked "Report Abuse" on every insulting post.

The next day at school, I tried to hold my head high as the girls walked by me and muttered "slut" and "whore" under their breath. I tried to talk to the creator of the drama and resolve our differences, but she didn't want to make up.

Those girls told me that I was worthless and that even before the fight, they'd had sleepovers solely for the purpose of making fun of me and that picture. I was at a loss for what to do. One night I slept over at the house of the only friend I had left. The next morning I woke up to dozens of text messages from kids in other towns whom the girls from my school had rallied against me.

Finally, after weeks and weeks of relentless torment, I cracked. I remember it distinctly: I was at an eye appointment, waiting for the doctor. My mom was there, playing on her phone. My own phone buzzed with a notification—yet another post on my Facebook wall. This one was no worse than the others, but I was so drained emotionally that I broke down in tears. Of course, at that point my mom got involved, which meant that the other girls' parents were notified. I wasn't happy that all the adults got entangled in the mess, but ultimately it was the only thing that stopped the cyberbullying.

A Bully's Confession

Michael Ortiz

Bully. Just the word makes me shudder. It's not a nice word any way you look at it. It doesn't give me strength or grant me protection from others. It's a dirty word. It's a word that marks me, that tells society I am evil. Mean-spirited.

I might as well have a "Kick Me" sign on my back, because being a bully doesn't save me from other bullies. I used to think that, somehow, tormenting others would grant me immunity from being tormented. It didn't. Because being a bully doesn't make you scary; it makes you worthless.

I am a self-confessed bully—well, a reformed one. Some people give me a look of disbelief when I say this. I'm not exactly what you imagine when you think *bully*: I'm short with curly hair and a high-pitched voice. I'm like Dill from *To Kill a Mockingbird*. I have a way with words, and it's my words that people fear. Though I hate to admit it, I can make a person hate themselves with a single word. I can evoke the nastiest, most secret insecurity that person has with one word. And it's that kind of bully we should fear most. Because what we secretly hate about ourselves can hurt us much more than what others think about us.

Digging up that dirt was my specialty. While other bullies were busy stealing lunch money on the playground, I was tearing people down to their roots, their very souls. And I didn't limit myself to those weaker and smaller; anyone who annoyed me was a target. Middle school—the beginning of what I call my "dark days"—turned me into a monster.

I like to say that, knowing the mind of a bully, there are actually three kinds: the bully who doesn't know what he's doing, the one who knows and can't stop it, and the bully who knows and doesn't want to stop it. I was the third one; I didn't want to stop ridiculing my peers because of the power. It's intoxicating to have so many people fear and respect you. The more people I bullied, the more grandiose I seemed to become.

Granted, I hated myself. I had always had issues with my identity, I felt self-conscious about my appearance, and I worried constantly about problems at home. It's a paradox, really. Bullies truly hate themselves. And it's this hate that makes the power of bullying so alluring, because, in a twisted way, instilling fear in others replaces the hate for oneself.

In seventh grade, some of my peers, sick of my tormenting, threatened to "jump" me. I was scared, truly scared, for the first time. At that point, I started thinking about my actions. I had gone so far down this path that I couldn't tell right from wrong anymore. I was stuck in a weird deadly dance, though I couldn't tell who my partner was, and I couldn't figure out if I was leading or being led. I had no control, no restraint, no temperance in my actions. And I hated myself.

I spent that summer crying, seeking direction. I didn't know what to do. Could I be a decent person? Did I have to put people down?

So, in eighth grade, I tried being a nice person. I didn't put people down, but the damage was done; only a fraction of my friends returned. And I couldn't blame the ones who didn't.

To those I tormented, I'm sorry. I'm so, so, so sorry. Words can't describe the remorse I feel, the nightmares my dark days give me. I know you still hate me, and that's okay. If I were you, I'd hate me too.

To my friends who stood by me as I found a new me, thank you. It's amazing that despite all the evil in my heart and all the harm I caused, you managed to find some good in me. It's because of you that I restarted life as a new man. A good man.

I regret my past, but it's the reason I am who I am now. My mother always says there are two sides of the world: a light side and a dark side. I'm living on the light side now, and let me tell you, it's beautiful. Straight paradise. The hate I once fostered in everyone, especially myself, was the dark side of my life, and I'm glad it's behind me.

Living Hell

Gwen Harrison

We moved when I was a kid, and I transferred to a new elementary school. In a day I went from a class of 35 to one of 15. Nobody acknowledged me except a brown-haired girl, Molly. She was new too, so we clicked immediately. A few of the kids teased me, but I assumed it would blow over. Little did I know that my role as a victim of bullying was being set and would follow me for the next seven years.

One girl, Andrea, came up to me and said, "Listen, new girl, I don't like you. I don't care that you're new. I don't want you here, and I don't want to get to know you. If you come back tomorrow, I'll make your life a living hell."

I was stunned. Molly told me to brush it off, so I tried, but Andrea's words echoed in my mind. I hoped that she was just joking.

The next day, Andrea and two friends cornered me in the hallway and began taunting me. "Hey, new girl! Where'd you get that hair bow? The trash?"

"Hey, new girl! When was the last time you washed your clothes?"

"That skirt is the ugliest thing I ever saw!" (I agreed with that, since we had to wear uniforms and the plaid skirts were dreadful. I found it ridiculous, though, that she was insulting my skirt when she was wearing the same one.)

The teasing was relentless, but somehow I didn't let it get to me. It was just these three girls, and I had Molly. Their words stung but didn't do any damage. Then things escalated. Andrea purposefully tripped me in gym class, resulting in a hairline fracture and sprained ankle.

My older sister, Amber, was being bullied too, and she had it even worse. The boys in her class picked on her because she was small. They vandalized her things, shoved her into walls, and verbally abused her. She spoke to the principal, who said she needed to toughen up, believing that she was making it up. When our mom finally talked to the principal, she promised she would take care of it, but still nothing changed.

Amber was facing another big hurdle. Her best friend and protector was diagnosed with cancer and passed away. She became depressed and suicidal, and when my mother found out, Amber was hospitalized.

I felt like everything in my life was spiraling out of control. I was in the fifth grade with a five-year-old sister, Ally, at home. I had to be strong for her and deal with my own bullying situation. I resorted to cutting and hid the scars under my volleyball jacket. This resulted in more bullying: "She must have a skin disease she's trying to cover up!" Things went from verbal to physical as the year continued. I was shoved into walls and pushed down stairs. My homework was shredded after I spent hours on it. Andrea left school, so I thought things would get better, but again I was wrong. Other bullies picked up right where she left off. Molly became a target too, because she was my friend.

In sixth grade, I finally complained to the school administration. Just like my sister, I was told to toughen up. I went to the principal again and again, hoping she'd help me, but nothing changed. So I intentionally failed two classes that I had excelled in, hoping my teacher would notice something was wrong. I skipped class, cut myself off from Molly, and stopped doing homework. I learned how to hide the fact that I was hurting.

In seventh grade, I hit my breaking point. One day I arrived at school early. I wanted to scream when I saw the classroom. The contents of my desk had been thrown all over the place, and my chair and desk were overturned. I began to put everything back, but as I picked up my papers, I saw that someone had written on them in big, red letters, "IF YOU COME TO SCHOOL TOMORROW, I WILL GO TO YOUR HOUSE AND KILL YOU!" "I WILL CHOKE YOU IN YOUR SLEEP!" "WHY DON'T YOU KILL YOURSELF SO WE CAN DANCE ON YOUR GRAVE?!" "GO TO HELL, YOU UGLY BITCH!"

I took these to my principal and demanded that something be done. She did something all right. She gave *me* a detention for "forging death threats"!

Feeling desperate, I broke down crying. I had tried everything, and even cutting wasn't relieving my pain anymore. I decided to do what my classmates wanted. I would commit suicide. I couldn't take it anymore. If nobody cared enough to help me, I might as well die.

That night when I was alone at home, I wrote two suicide notes—one to my family, the other for my school—describing everything that had been happening since second grade. I blamed the teachers and students who either bullied me or watched and did nothing. I held nothing back. I closed the letter with, "I hope you're happy. You got what you wanted. Now I hope you can live with it."

I grabbed a bottle of painkillers and dumped a bunch into my hand. I was shaking. I thought about the pain finally ending. Suddenly I realized that by ending my life, I would be causing enormous pain for those who loved me. Molly. My sisters. My parents, who never even knew I was struggling with the same issues as my older sister. Mrs. B, the only teacher who took an interest in me.

I held my life in my hands in that moment, and I couldn't do it. I couldn't put my loved ones through that. I flushed the pills, crumpled up the notes, and hid in my room, sobbing. I was up all night. The next day at school, after my usual lunchtime torture, I broke down. None of the bullies had ever seen me cry, but I didn't care anymore. I needed help.

Mrs. B came into the room and saw me with my head down on my desk. She took me into the hallway and sat me on the stairs. She rolled up my sleeves to reveal my cut-up arms and saw my tear-streaked face. In that moment, she understood how serious the situation was.

She made me tell her everything. Who was tormenting me. When. What they said and did. How long it had been going on. I poured my heart out. She nodded sympathetically and took notes. In almost a whisper, I told her about my breakdown the previous night, making her swear not to report me. "I can't put my family through this. Not again. Not after what happened to Amber."

She nodded and said, "Never in my thirty years of teaching have I seen two students nearly end their lives because of bullying. I can't believe that both you and your sister had to endure this and nothing was done. I promise this will never happen again. To you or any other student."

Too bad the kids on my bus didn't hear her, because they beat me up on the way home that day. I finally told my mom that I needed to get out of that school as soon as possible. Summer was a few weeks away, so we visited some other schools that I might attend that fall. I had a black eye from the bus, but I cut my bangs to hide it.

Usually an outgoing person, I was withdrawn on this visit. Then a girl ran up and welcomed me warmly. After that I decided that this school was right for me. I moved on without ever looking back.

Now, as a sophomore, I have threatened many bullies. I am feared in my new school—not as a bully but as a guardian. I will forever be an advocate for bullying prevention. My previous school finally cracked down on bullying shortly after I left, expelling eight students, two of whom had made me their victim.

My bullies still don't know the impact they had on my life. I've been asked if I want revenge. I simply reply, "Why should I take revenge on someone who made me stronger?"

Vultures

Nicole Rossi

Vultures. Tormentors.
Monsters in pain
Preying on helplessness
Living in shame

Vicious young ladies
Insecure with themselves
Their brow-beating's really
A sick call for help

Screwed up in the mind
And starving for change
Ravenous for praise
For attention, for fame

You're fat
And you're ugly
You're worthless; you're trash
They pass on these thoughts
To the ones they harass

And nobody wins
But the self-doubting mind

That dark, evil demon
Can be so unkind

The bullies, they really
Can't see what they do
Can't see hating themselves
Makes them hate others too

So take pity on them
The savage young beasts
Rise above their cruel words
Indulge in the feast

The feast that is knowing
You're strong and secure
You are good enough
Even when you're unsure

And fill up on truth
And drink to your scars
For they're what make you
The person you are

The vultures will feed
Rip bodies to shreds
But they will not satisfy
Their insatiable dread

And if one of them catches you
Don't run away
Try to feed them some truth
They might change their cruel ways

And don't settle for worthless
For self-doubt and pain
And know that you, too
Will be whole again

Pushed Too Far

Caitlyn Hannon

"You stupid lesbo," he says as he pushes me into a row of lockers. Panic panic. "You're so stupid," he sneers. "I saw you kiss her. Why did you do that?" He tries to trip me. Oh God, where is an adult when I need one?

I guess I should have seen it coming. I was stupid for letting myself fall into this trap.

It's sophomore year, and I'm in my school's musical. After rehearsal one evening I'm waiting in the stairwell for my brother to finish crew. I'm working on some geometry problems when this guy sits down next to me. I don't know his name, but I've seen him hanging around.

"What are you doing?" he asks.

"My homework," I answer, without looking at him.

"That's boring. C'mon, let's go for a walk," he says, standing up. I know I shouldn't. He has never been particularly nice to me. But for some reason I get up.

We start walking down the darkened hallways, making small

talk, until I realize that we are in an empty corridor out of earshot of any adults. That's when he corners me.

"Do you fight?" he asks. I don't quite know what he means.

"I'm really more passive-aggressive," I answer slowly. That's when he starts pushing me and bringing up an exchange he witnessed between me and a friend.

Then he's messing up my hair. "There, now it matches the rest of you," he laughs smugly. "So are you really a lesbo? Or are you bi?"

"Neither. I'm straight," I answer meekly. He shakes his head and grins evilly.

"Then why did you kiss a girl? She's hot and you're not," he states, like it's an obvious fact that ugly girls and pretty girls should never kiss. And I'm not. Ugly, that is.

"Look, it was just a peck on the lips. Lots of girls kiss hello and good-bye nowadays, genius," I shoot back. I see the look in his eyes, and my stomach sinks as I realize, *Now I'm gonna get it.*

We're in a stairwell now, and he grabs me around the waist, trying to push me down the stairs. "I should just lock you out in the rain so your hair frizzes," he grunts as he struggles with me. "Then you'll feel as ugly as you are."

Luckily we're about the same size, so I plant my feet firmly and manage to maintain my balance. He gives up and instead tries to toss me into a corner. I push him away and start walking quickly toward the main hallway where there are bound to be other people. *Breathe. Look strong. Don't annoy him.*

He comes up behind me as I turn down a hall that leads to the main corridor. I can see the shapes of people passing by at the other end. It's like the light guiding me to heaven, my salvation.

"I could smack your ass right now and you wouldn't do anything," he baits.

"Yes, I would," I declare as I plow forward, because what can I say: "You're right, I won't defend myself against sexual harassment"? Then I feel his hand smack my behind, and my temper ignites. I whirl around, grabbing his arms and pinning them to his sides.

"Don't. You. Ever. Do. That. Again," I growl through clenched teeth. He smirks and shakes free. I turn and push through the doors to the hallway and have never been so relieved to be among others.

I grab my brother and we go home. I don't cry until I get in my room. My mom hears my sobs, however, and comes in to soothe me.

"I wasn't strong," I cry in her arms. "I didn't fight back. I know you taught me to never let a guy boss me around, but I couldn't stand up for myself!"

She pats my hair and calms me down. "Sometimes sticking up for yourself means using your brain, not your brawn. Think about what would have happened if you had punched him. He could have seriously hurt you, and you both would be in trouble. But you didn't give him that chance. You used your head and got yourself to a safe place. That takes strength too," she says. I go to bed with this thought in my head.

When I see him in the halls the next day, I hold my breath, wondering what he's going to do. We pass each other without a word or even a glance. It's like nothing happened.

I exhale in relief. I head to Spanish class and slide into my desk next to my friend and start chatting, as though I wasn't threatened last night. I tell myself I've grown from this experience. I realize now that by being strong and brave I got myself safely out of a bad situation. And that's something to be proud of.

© 2013 Maya Gouw

Pride and Prejudice

Hillel Zand

I'm proud of being Jewish, but when the cruel jokes began in high school, I started to question everything I'd ever been told about my faith and culture.

"Hey, I found a penny," said a friend. Then, as he threw it into the dirt, he yelled, "Go fetch!"

"That's so Jewish" became a favorite among my friends too. About half the time when I say something about money, "That's so Jewish" follows, even after I insist for the umpteenth time that it's not funny.

I'll admit, I wasn't always aware of how offensive jokes about religion can be. I have a friend who's Mormon. I used to occasionally make polygamy jokes until he vehemently insisted that I stop. Once I realized how much it bothered him, I didn't make another joke about his religion. Why can't my friends give me the same courtesy and respect?

I come from a loving home that accepts all backgrounds. We are proud to be Jewish but don't flaunt our religion. Judaism (and religion in general) isn't a topic I typically discuss with my friends, even though I'd be glad to have a serious conversation with them about our respective faiths. But to them my religion and heritage is simply fodder for hurtful and derogatory jokes. They don't bother to learn anything about it. That's what annoys me the most.

Some have argued that a person's religion is a choice, and that if I don't like being taunted for being Jewish, I should convert. To me, that's absurd. No matter how much anti-Semitism I experience, I will always be a Jew. Judaism is my culture, my belief system, the root of my morals and ethics. It's so much more than they will ever understand, and I wouldn't change it for anything.

My only wish is that people, especially my less-mature friends, would take the time to learn about how anti-Semitic ideas and actions have led to devastating results throughout history. Jews have been persecuted since the Exodus, and the burdens that come with our tragic but proud heritage can be a lot to handle. Let's face it: being a minority can suck sometimes. But that's reality.

What may seem like harmless slurs and jokes can be dangerous. The first step to ending religious discrimination is education—education about what history has proven can happen when ignorance and intolerance go unchecked. Making an effort to understand other cultures and speaking up against discrimination are both parts of that education.

Sympathy for the Devil

Jack Bentele

It might be a cliché: I entered middle school doe-eyed and doughy, ready to face the exciting prospects of almost high school. Alas, I was cut down by a bully during the horror known as gym class. Little things, like pushes and shoves into locker doors, slowly broke down my resolve. Every day, sixth period ruined my life.

Here, though, is where I learned the rules: toughen up, don't tattle, know your place in the pecking order. I wasn't one of the "cool" kids, one of the athletes, or even one of the respected nerds. The bullying didn't happen because I was being singled out, and that's the most damaging part about it. I was interchangeable with all the other invisible kids. Thrown into this environment where parents and teachers no longer rule, kids build their own hierarchy, and if your role is to get pushed around and ignored, you might as well not exist at all.

In this purgatory, I wandered from hall to hall, class to class, arranging my life around sixth period—gym class—and the dominating figure of my bully.

Looking back now, he seems a lot smaller. Many years have passed, and I have toughened up. I'm bothered by other problems now, but they are more existential and pretentious these days. With the help of the people who love me, I made it through middle school. Yet when I think back, I still feel the dents in my armor. What that bully did lasted.

Then I discovered through Facebook that the all-powerful bully of my past recently took his own life. How am I supposed to feel about that? It's not like I knew him well; after sixth grade, it was almost as if nothing had ever happened between us. Even though he affected my life in so many ways, I wonder if I had any impact on his. It's strange to think that I, who feared him every day, was probably a very minuscule part of his life. To him I truly was invisible.

Yet it seems like I was the lucky one after all. The small ways he abused me in middle school were tiny blips in the larger context of his life, his struggles. I was an outlet, and even though he injured me, it doesn't make him a malicious force. Underneath it all, he was a poor, confused kid like me. For a brief few months, our lives brushed against each other in that locker room and then drifted apart just as easily.

Bullying isn't some great mystery. Middle school can be one of the worst, most heartbreaking times. Naturally, people are going to have problems. Those problems create both the bullies and the bullied. We're all products of our environment, and we all need kindness and hope during that challenging period. I was lucky; I had the support of my parents and friends.

But who did my bully have?

The Solitary
Jenica Jessen

you see them
in the corners
in the crannies of the lunchroom
you see them
alone
sitting with their backpacks
alone

and they eat quickly
racing the clock so they
can run to the library
they eat quickly so they
can go back into hiding
in the pages of a book
or behind a computer monitor

and they hunch over their food like
a small wild animal
that wants to finish before
its dinner is taken away
by something bigger

like a small wild animal
that must eat
before it is eaten
and they curl up into themselves

when strangers
(everyone)
pass by
like they are worried
that someone will interrupt them

or even worse
that nobody will

and they stare at the table
like they don't want to be seen
they stare silently at the table
or dart quick glances around the room
the roaring rowdy room
like they're being watched

they aren't

Devin Scott's Story

Megan Haddox

Tuesday, August 7, 2012, will forever be a day my senior class will remember with heavy hearts. It's the day we lost a member of our class to suicide as a result of bullying.

On August 6, the second day of school, Devin Scott bumped into another student and gave him the finger. The other kid wanted to fight. When Devin went home instead of going to the park to fight, the boy and fifty other students went to Devin's house and stood outside chanting his name and saying mean things.

Devin tried to call the police but couldn't get through on the nonemergency line. He didn't think he should call 911 because he didn't need an ambulance. Devin also called our school's resource officer. That night after the students left his house, Devin was mocked on Facebook for not fighting. The next day at school, he and the other boy met with an officer to discuss the situation.

Devin was a friend to many, an acquaintance to some, a smiling face in the hallway to all. Then in an instant he was gone.

When his family got home that day, kids were again outside the house yelling that Devin was a coward for not fighting. His parents told the kids to go home or they would call the cops. When his parents entered the house, they found Devin's body. Overcome with shock and grief, Devin's mother came outside in tears and screamed at the kids that Devin had killed himself.

That night, everyone heard the sad news on Facebook. Our class decided to wear blue in memory of Devin. It was shocking to see how many took part, especially given how many kids had been at Devin's house just the night before, taunting him.

Our school held a candlelight memorial. Devin's family attended and thanked everyone for coming together to remember Devin. As the theme song from the movie *Up* played, we released blue balloons with messages to Devin written on them. Many students shared stories of how Devin had saved them from suicide, or that, even though they didn't know him, they were devastated a student could be bullied to death. As people shared their stories, a light rain began to fall. We felt that, even though Devin wasn't with us anymore, he was crying with us.

Since Devin's death, bullying isn't as common at my school, but as in any high school, if you look for it, you will find it. It's really sad that we had to lose a student before anyone implemented a real plan to address bullying. My only hope is that this will never happen again, here or anywhere.

We Can't All Be "In"

Kaitlyn Blais

Kids are cruel—there's no doubt about that. There's something about the early teenage years that makes young people seek validation through others. They want to be cool, popular, and "in." The problem is that you can't be "in" unless someone is "out." Forget being popular; just to be accepted as normal there must be a black sheep to be compared against.

Sixth grade was one of the worst years of my life, socially speaking. We had just moved to a new neighborhood, and I had several strikes against me before I even stepped into school. I stood out too much. It was a kindergarten through sixth-grade school, so most of my class had known each other since they were five. And I was also the only kid who wasn't black. I was an outsider in many ways.

After several failed attempts at making friends, I opted to just keep my head down and stick to my books. I was initially teased about my "boy" hair and for being a nerd, but when I ignored them they eventually left me alone.

It was easy to find the other black sheep in class. His name was Daniel. He stood a full six inches above everyone else and had a terrible stutter. No one hid their eye-rolling when Daniel tried to join in their conversation.

I assumed Daniel had been targeted for years, but he never gave up trying to be accepted. It was much more rewarding for our peers to bully him than me, because he reacted. When kids asked Daniel, "Why are you so slow, stupid?" He would stutter something about telling his mom or the teacher, and everyone would roar with laughter. I swear I even saw the teacher snicker once or twice. Eventually I grew tired of sitting by and watching kids torment him.

I can't quite remember what they were saying to Daniel that day, but it infuriated me. I stood up, poked the ringleader in the chest, and shouted, "Do you really have nothing better to do than pick on someone who obviously just wants to be your friend?"

That was when they focused their racial jokes and harassment on me.

We all know what happens when a person is bullied, so I won't go into detail, but I want to tell you what happened to Daniel. He was no longer bullied; instead, he was basically ignored after I stood up for him. Indirectly, I did eventually help him make friends, though. You see, Daniel realized that he could bond with his classmates by joining in humiliating me.

To my complete surprise, they accepted him. By joining the side of the bullies, he crossed the line from "out" to "in." He and I both learned that there needed to be only one black sheep— and it wasn't him anymore.

Chapter Two

SURVIVE IT

*"Believe that life is worth living
and your belief will help create the fact."*

—William James

Befriending My Bully

Jaemin (Joseph) Lee

When I was 10 and realized I was attracted to men, I decided to tell my mother. Despite being from Korea, a very conservative country, she had no issues with my being gay. Yet I often saw her cry at night. When I asked why, she explained she worried about my safety in a society that demonizes homosexuality. I didn't think much about her words then, but as I grew up, I began to understand.

In my middle school, a typical conversation between the boys went something like this:

"Yo! What's up?"

"Hey. Just reading."

"That's gay."

"Yeah, it is."

"Let's go do something less gay, man. Stop being a fag."

When I realized these boys were using "gay" as a derogatory term, I was confused. What's so wrong with liking a boy? And why would reading make someone gay? I felt a sense of being disowned by society at 11, but I also believed that anyone who said things like this must be pretty ignorant.

In high school, the bullying reached an all-time high. I lived in an all-boys dorm, and the other 14-year-olds constantly laughed about gay people, sexualized women, and made other jokes that I found disconcerting. Boys would pretend to be gay with one another, which they found hilarious. Once they figured out I was gay, some refused to speak to me, others would laugh at me or try to entice me and then laugh at me, and others simply watched.

One of my worst bullies was a kid I'll call Max. Max was large and easily fit in, since he played football. I knew he wasn't a bad kid at heart, and I believed he played up his hatred of gay people to fit in. When Max asked me to wrestle him (another thing that freshman boys did), I was eager to take him down.

Weirdly, I really believed I could beat Max, and I did. I caught his head in my arms and entangled my body around him so he couldn't move. I guess those figure skating and ballet lessons paid off. These boys marveled at physical strength, and because I had overpowered the biggest kid, they were amazed. I think they were particularly impressed because they had grown up being told that gay men are feminine and weak.

That was one good moment, but to be honest, my life was horrible. I was constantly ostracized and told I didn't belong. But I knew that the most important thing I could do was change the way people thought. I needed to teach not only these boys but every intolerant person at my school that all people are multidimensional and unique. That's when I decided I was not going to go to war with my peers, nor was I going to run away. I was going to befriend them and show them that I was more than a stereotype: more than anything, I was human.

When I realized that all I needed to do was have them see me for who I was, it didn't take much to make friends. I was funny, I danced, I played computer games competitively. My peers grew to like me, but more than that, they learned to look past my sexual orientation.

A few years later, Max and I even became friends. It started with him trying to get me to join the football team. He would say, "So, I know a bunch of coaches who want you to join," or "Dude, you would be awesome at football. I've never had anyone take me down like you did." Though it could have been a good chance to show people how multidimensional I was, I just wasn't interested.

Then one day I was surprised when I found Max at choir rehearsal. I remember he just came in and casually said, "What's up?" Meanwhile, I was thinking, *What the heck is this jock doing here?*

It turned out he had a great voice, and we got to know each other better and became friends. One day we started talking about freshman year.

Me: "Remember how freshman year we didn't have to work at all?"

Max: "Wait, I always thought you were studying in your room."

Me: "No way, man. I was playing computer games. I just didn't like going out 'cause, uh . . . you know."

Max: "Oh, I forgot all about that. Wow, I didn't think you'd actually not want to leave your room because of us."

Me: "Well, it was pretty bad for me."

Max: "Dude, I was so stupid then. I'm really sorry. I didn't realize how much it was hurting you, but I also knew I was being a real jerk."

Me: "Yeah . . . It's cool though. Thanks for apologizing."

Max: "Who else bullied you?"

Me: "Colin, Sam, John . . . But the worst was that none of the teachers helped me. No one really was on my side."

Max: "I didn't know it was that bad! I was such an asshole."

Me: "Yeah."

Max: "Dude, who was the worst?"

Me: "You were pretty bad, but Julius was bad too. He told me to go hang myself."

Max: "What the hell? Well, screw him."

I began to see Max as more than the guy who had bullied me freshman year. Interestingly, the other boys would later tell me they were sorry.

I never thought at the beginning of my freshman year that by junior year these boys would sincerely apologize. It took me by surprise. My experiences with Max proved my belief in the multidimensional nature of people. I think the best part about him, though, is that he was able to take a step outside of his "masculinity zone," defying the stereotypes that society had placed even on him.

I like to think that I helped other kids understand that doing what you want and trying new things doesn't have to be limited by gender roles, age, or especially society. These people will hopefully keep this understanding and eventually teach it to their children. Then it will be worth enduring any pain on my part. I was constantly bullied and hurt, but despite that, or perhaps thanks to it, I was able to help make a more tolerant world.

I still live in an intolerant society that can be even worse than the bullying I faced at school. Sometimes it's from a radical Christian priest or a conservative teacher, but it is inevitable that I face discrimination. However, in this struggle, I find benefits: the satisfaction of knowing that if I live and work to the best of my abilities, I can help others develop into more tolerant and accepting people.

King Worm

Robert Hwang

I stared out into the golden horizon, watching a parade of sunlight blink across the surface of the water. It was that magical time when the sun pokes its head up from the horizon, signaling the start of a new day. The morning air filled my lungs as I breathed the satisfying color of blue that you can smell only around water.

It was just me and my papa that morning, standing on the sandy bank of a lake, the water's edge splish-splashing a few feet away. My pole was in my hands, and my eyes were fixed on the tiny circle where the line disappeared beneath the surface of the water. The line remained motionless, waiting to snag a fish.

But my head was stuck in the past, stuck in a time when the smell of hatred lingered, and the reservoir of vengeance was waiting to be filled. *Nobody knows*, I told myself. *I'm the only one.*

My pole started to shake, and I jumped. I shook myself from my daze and reeled the line in furiously, but when the hook popped out of the water, it was empty. A lost worm.

"How many times do I have to tell you?" my dad snapped. "When you feel it go down, the fish is biting and you have to set the hook. Pay attention."

"I know, I'm sorry," I replied.

My dad didn't talk much, and when he did, it was mostly to scold me for what I had done or tell me what I should have done.

Still, I wanted him to know what was on my mind. I knew he would yell and criticize me for my mistakes, but I wanted to gather the strength to tell him my story.

I reached into the bait container and grabbed another plump worm, crushing it in half with my thumb. It reminded me of myself when I was a kid. Vulnerable. Defeated. I was a worm, or at least I felt like it.

And some people really hate worms.

My childhood enemy was Eric. He was one of those arrogant, overprivileged types, but one thing that always stood out to me was his devilish smile. I hated that smile because it meant he was up to no good.

One time in third grade the class was lining up to wait for the buses to take us home. Most days I avoided Eric, but that day, unfortunately, I was lined up near him and his group of cronies. I was wearing a yellow polo my mom had bought for me, with the letters "LBBJ" across the breast pocket.

Eric was laughing with his friends. I remember thinking, *Please don't look my way*, but it did me no good. He and his friends spotted me and marched over like a bunch of thugs.

"Hey, what's that?" He pointed at the letters on my shirt.

"LBBJ? Does that mean Little Baby Butt Junior?"

"N-no!" I stuttered. My face reddened.

I tried to act cool, but he could sense my fear. His expression turned bleak, and that familiar, devilish smile appeared on his face. Nobody would help me. I knew this, and so did he.

Heart pumping, I bolted for the other side of the hall. But I was too slow, and one of his cronies caught me around the waist and shoved me back toward Eric.

"You can't hurt me," I said, trying to sound courageous.

"Can't hurt you?" Eric snickered. "Wanna bet?"

Before I could reply, he cocked his arm and launched a fierce uppercut into my belly, forcing the breath from my lungs. The burning sensation seemed to seep into my skin, engulfing my body. It was the kind of punch that has a lingering aftertaste.

When I got home, I took off the yellow polo shirt and furiously stuffed it into the depths of my closet, vowing never to wear it again. That punch stayed with me all night, as I lay in bed soaking my pillow with tears of regret.

I was powerless to stop the bullying, and because of that I became absorbed in meaningless self-pity. I pitied myself; I hated those who made me feel like a worthless worm. And most of all, I pitied my life.

When I was little, my family moved to this small town in Missouri to open a family Chinese restaurant. I hated almost every moment living in that place. Though my parents were oblivious to it, the city had a faint whiff of prejudice. I always felt different, like a foreigner. The burning heat of racism constantly surrounded my life at school. My parents were too busy with their restaurant to notice. And ironically, I didn't want them to know that I was too afraid to tell an adult about it.

So I wandered around every day like a sardine in a school of whitefish. During my time in that school system, I saw only a few kids of color, and that whiff of prejudice would become stronger when they were around. Many of them didn't stay for long, and I always thought they were the lucky ones. When they left, the sad thing was, nobody cared. It was like they were instantly forgotten. I always wished I would be the next to leave, but the family business took priority. I knew there was nothing I could do, and being teased and pushed around was so normal that I associated school with bullying.

Desperate to find a way to deal with the bullying, I decided to become a bully myself.

It was a gradual change, like how milk turns sour as it warms up. I sat back quietly and watched the many Erics doing their thing, carefully observing the secrets to being a bully. I was tired of waiting for results; I wanted change.

I decided to become the King Worm, the one nobody would pick on without facing punishment. I copied the attitude of my bullies and began to torment other helpless victims.

I soon commanded my own group of cronies. I used my brains to outsmart the teachers; a friendly game of tag in their view was a perfect opportunity to push someone to the ground, or a little race on the playground was a cover-up to trip an unsuspecting victim.

Ironically, I made a lot of friends this way. People started to respect and fear me. Other bullies even stopped teasing me. I had won acceptance, but it was not the satisfying life I hoped for. But I did not give up, and one day a new kid named Adam arrived.

He was white, which was no surprise, with freckles below his heavy eyelids and a big pair of buck teeth that protruded past his lips. His face was almost rabbitlike. When asked to read in class, he stuttered horribly.

How embarrassing. I chuckled. *An easy target,* I thought.

"Hey, Adam," I said during recess. "Follow me. We're going to have some fun."

I led the way; Adam followed quietly. Near the back of the playground was an area we called The Hill. It was just steep enough that nobody could see you at the bottom, and because of that, teachers told students to avoid the area. But the teachers were somewhere else, so I took Adam down The Hill.

There, I turned around and said, "You're the new kid here, and I don't like you."

I glared at him with deadly eyes. He was hopeless, a nobody at the bottom of the hierarchy.

As soon as he turned to run, my hand clenched into a ball.

I hesitated, but then I did it anyway. My fist struck out quickly and grated into his upper back.

Adam let out a startled cry, loud enough to turn the heads of a few kids, but not loud enough to alert the teachers.

He ran off without a word.

After that, I made Adam my special victim, shoving my

knuckles into his back throughout the day. *Pick on the weak, and you won't get picked on yourself,* I thought.

One day when I got home, I found a letter addressed to me in the mailbox. It was from Adam's dad, and it contained a picture of Adam's exposed back, covered in red marks. I was forced to face my mistakes head on.

Now, at the lake with my dad, I looked at my hand covered in worm guts. The plump worm writhed in my grip as I stabbed it on to the hook. It continued to squirm, trying to escape the steel skewering its flesh.

I looked at my dad, thinking again about telling him. I wanted him to know everything. I wanted to tell him about how I had been punched because I was Asian, kicked because I had no friends, and spat on because I tried to resist. I wanted to tell him why I had become a monster myself.

But I didn't. His sad brown eyes were peering deep into the lake as if they knew all too well. I cast my line out into the shining sun, and the worm danced in the watery depths, hoping for another chance to catch that fish.

Rhino Skin

Sarah Hamel

If I had to choose one game to describe my life, it would be Telephone. The rules are simple: a sentence is whispered from one person to the next to see just how much it changes by the time it gets to the last person.

My life is a schoolwide game of Telephone. Some stories start off stupid enough to make me laugh, and some become too absurd for words. But however it's distorted, gossip spreads carelessly, and mending the damage takes patience and hard work. Every day I want to grab a megaphone and shout: "What you heard was wrong! Call this number to find out all my real secrets!"

There's no getting around it—there will always be mean teenagers. But it is possible to develop a defense against bullying. I have. My mom calls it my rhino skin.

I'll be honest: hearing the word "dyke" shouted down the hall and realizing it was meant for me stung at first. How could it not? But the more I'm called a name, the sillier it starts to sound coming out of someone's mouth. Why should I care what these people think?

Sometimes I even embrace the labels. My two best friends and I call ourselves the Three Whores, and I'm Number One. The word means nothing to us anymore.

Pothead. Tease. Whore. Dork. Nag. Bossy. Weird. Geek. God-hater. Slut. Dyke. Tranny. Brat. Attention-whore. Awkward. Cheater. Bitch. Anorexic. Hypocrite. Faggot. Retard. Liar.

These are the words I've become immune to—the ones that bounce off my rhino skin. I have my own version of that old saying: sticks and stones may break my bones, but words will eventually stop hurting me after I get used to them.

I'm not going to lie and say that ignoring gossip and teasing is easy and painless. It's not. But I had no choice in high school. A group of nice teachers or a peer mediator club will never have a big enough impact to make bullying go away. If they can't even stop teens from smoking, how are they going to stop them from judging?

Teenagers live in a world of false assumptions and exaggerated criticism. All we targets can do is find the strength to shield ourselves from the words. We toughen up our rhino skin until the bad stuff can't penetrate, and just lumber on.

If We Were Allies

Kaylee Euler

Every day is the same. Every single day of my life is the same hell, as if my world is stuck on repeat. Sure, each time the movie plays, a few new details are added. Maybe it isn't a movie but a thousand revisions of a novel, a never-ending editing process. The words are tweaked, but the plot remains the same.

My hair is dyed, my skin concealed. My voice is perfectly pitched to match theirs. But no matter how I try to change myself to fit in, my tormentors find new scabs to pick raw.

Dignity seems like a foreign word that I've long since forgotten. I'll do anything to avoid their jabs. Pride—that's gone too, along with my hope of normalcy or fitting in.

Today, I sit alone in the cafeteria, as usual. Most students are outside with friends, basking in the sunshine. I don't care for sun, nor do I have friends to sit with.

A small group of other outsiders sits across the cafeteria, shooting me dark glares. I know they're not interested in me for anything other than staring or scheming some nasty prank. I watch them from under my messy blonde-from-a-box bangs. They don't eat, too worried about their image. It's disgusting how boney these girls are. They used to look normal, healthy, and beautiful.

Of course, I've changed too. They try to achieve perfection through their weight; I too strive to fit in. We are the same. Will my next attempt to fit in be to look like that? The thought sickens me, and yet there it is.

I realize something. They aren't outside either. That little group of five used to be the socialites, always with the in crowd. Now they're here with me. They too have been exiled.

If all the weak, pitiful exiles worked together, what would we be? Surely there are others here who have been pushed to the borders of the social sphere. I scan the room. A lone pair sits in the shadowy corner—the Harris twins. As I look around me, more and more of us emerge.

We are the outcasts. We're weak alone. We have no power when we are separated. But today the plot of the novel has changed. What if we joined forces? If we were allies, we could topple the in crowd, easily outnumbering them. Their empire would fall, bringing peace once and for all.

We could be strong. We could end this war of hatred.

Slowly, I stand and walk toward the small group who had been staring at me. The twins follow close behind.

I Forgive You

Grace Park

Dear Anonymous Stranger,

I think about you a lot. I deleted my Facebook account, but in my mind I can still see all the thumbs-up "likes" that your comment got. I don't check my phone at school, but I imagine pixelated usernames floating above heads in the hallways—above strangers and former friends. The familiar cliques and couples are now matrices of glowing dots spun around in cruel words with usernames that all "liked" your comment.

Somehow, stranger hidden behind a screen, you turned my life upside down with just one comment. What you posted, harshly and anonymously, told me this (and I almost believed it):

> **Something to Fear**
> I don't have
> true friends that love me no matter what.
> I'm surrounded by
> those who judge and sneer.

And I know who's at fault:
myself—and only myself.
It's true that the person in control is
you, not me.
The person without friends is
a loser who's not worth anything.
No one really thinks that I'm
brave enough to stand up for myself.
People believe that I'm
too weak to be anyone important.
It's a lie that I can be
someone I'm proud of.
I'm capable of being
that loser, that's all.
I wish I could help
myself and be strong.
I know I will eventually accept
that I deserve to be bullied.
I will never believe . . .

Whatever your comment may have said about me, it told me more about you. It told me that you think you're safe behind your mask of secret accounts.

Let me tell you something, stranger: I can trace every single thing you've written about me back to you. I can follow every keystroke and emoticon you used back to a person who's just as lonely as you claim I am—a person who's more afraid of being a loser, a loner, a nobody-special than I am. And now that I know that heartbreaking truth, I'm not afraid of you. Being anonymous doesn't mean being brave. Being anonymous means being alone.

So, anonymous, lonely stranger, I'll take your messages and trace them back to you. I'll catch your hand as it's about to click "send" and hold it close to my heart as we trace back every Instagram and text you've ever sent. I'll hold your hand in mine until, in the end, when our fingers point back to you, they don't point accusingly toward someone who's just as lost as me. Instead, our hands, intertwined, will spread their fingers out to someone else next to us, and we'll read them what you told me, backward.

I will never believe . . .
that I deserve to be bullied.
I know I will eventually accept
Myself and be strong.
I wish I could help
That loser, that's all.
I'm capable of being
Strong.
It's a lie that I can be
too weak for anyone to care.
People believe that I'm
good enough to stand up for myself.
No one really thinks that I'm
a loser who can't fit in.
The person without friends is

you, not me.
It's true that the person in control is
myself—and only myself.
And I know who's at fault:
those who judge and sneer.
I'm surrounded by
true friends who love me no matter what.
I don't have
Something to Fear

Dear stranger holding my hand, I forgive you.

Unfriendly Fire

Jordan Molineux

As a "military brat," I've had the opportunity to witness human nature on an international scale. Consequently, I've seen many forms of love, hate, friendship, and sorrow. One thing that translates into any language and culture is, unfortunately, bullying. It's a human response to insecurity and lack of control, a magician's trick to divert attention from one's own flaws by showcasing another's. Bullying and I go way back.

I lived for ten months in a small Alabama town, where I was judged by the middle school populace. The jury found me guilty of every charge. Since I'm oddly pale, the local bullies called me a vampire. I wore black twice, I must be emo. I held hands with my friend for two seconds, I'm a lesbian. The list grew. When I wasn't being teased, I was either invisible or a ghost—you saw me, I existed, but I wasn't alive unless I was with friends. I let myself be a cliché.

When it all started, I tried to turn the other cheek, not to react. But the kids kept pouring pack after pack of Mentos into the liter of Coke, wanting me to erupt. Next I tried being passive-aggressive, using dirty looks as ammunition when they prodded me with verbal abuse. I tried being aggressive, angrily telling them not to touch me when we were on the soccer field. The bullying became more of a game to them. I was the one who wouldn't cry for them, but that didn't stop them from trying.

I fought them in my thoughts, wondering why they were being so cruel and immature when I hadn't said a word to provoke them. Even after it became clear we weren't going to sit

around braiding each other's hair and getting matching tattoos, I was willing to draw up a treaty and start at square one. Still, the abuse persisted.

After one of my tormentors gave me an absentminded compliment one

© 2013 Grace Elizabeth Stathos

day, I realized that they weren't even targeting me specifically, at least not all the time. I was simply one of the many they messed with to get a laugh out of their friends. I was the means to an end: to prove they were bold. They wanted to be the type of girl others looked at in awe and said, "Did she really say that?"

Before those ten months, I was an outgoing, happy person.

After those ten months, I felt as though that younger, more naive me had committed suicide. Now I know what was necessary for me to become my own hero. I learned how to be real with those girls. I needed to strip away the emotional fuel I gave them and tell them what I was thinking and how their actions made me lose respect for them. I needed to own up to who I was and walk away with my newfound superpowers.

Nobody's Power

Megan LaColla Linquist

I hear the over-enunciated T of people's whispered sluT

I hear the harshness of the K when I become the definition
   of freaK

I feel the breeze of the WH when the wind carries to me
   the word WHore

I feel the punch of the CH when people cough into their
   hands that I'm the synonym of a female dog

You say I am nobody

But all these words, they must have to specify someone,
   be meant for someone.

I know they are meant for me because I can taste the blood
   on my lip from the CH punch, the goosebumps from
   the WH breeze are tangible

And you know I am too

because I see the bruises on your knuckles from the punch

I see your chapped lips from all the talk

I feel your energy dwindling as you silently hand me
   your power,

the power to

not care

Standing Up for Simone

Damiana B. Andonova

Unfortunately, being bullied runs in my family.

When we immigrated to America many years ago, I was bullied for my accent and for eating ethnic food for lunch. My classmates took advantage of my poor English and tricked me by giving me the wrong definition of swear words, which got me into trouble with teachers. In junior high, I was called a lesbian because I held another girl's hand—which is customary in my home country of Bulgaria.

My parents' advice proved ineffective—ignoring the teasing made it worse, and saying "Thank you for your opinion" didn't work either. If I told the teacher, I was a tattletale, and sarcastic comebacks like "I must be really interesting if you're talking about me all the time" didn't stop the barrage of insults. I was called an FOB ("fresh off the boat"), a weirdo, fat, and a know-it-all.

My persecution was annoying, but eventually I was too busy volunteering, studying, and babysitting to let it get to me. By junior year in high school, it was over.

For me, anyway.

My sister, Simone, who was six at the time, was becoming less and less eager to go to school. She would lie about being sick and dawdle getting ready in the morning. When she talked about girls being "sassy," I didn't pay attention. Neither did my parents.

Then she came home crying one day and told us that some girls in her class pushed her every day, knocked her books to the floor, and excluded her at recess. When we advised her to tell the teacher, they told her to stop "tattling." It took a bruise on her forehead for the school to get involved. Nonetheless, the other girl's parents denied that she was at fault.

When it became clear that the school would not protect Simone, I skipped school to visit her classroom. Appalled by what I saw, I told my parents we had to find her another school that took bullying seriously.

When we visited another school and met the principal, I grilled him about their academic policies, teacher credentials, and bullying-prevention programs. Simone's only question was, "I am not going to be bullied here, right?" When Simone was bullied again, her new school reacted faster and resolved the issues before much damage was done.

Removing Simone from her original school helped initially. But four years later, it is more than obvious to us, her family, and her teachers that bullying continues to affect her. Bullying may stop, but its impact on the victim's socio-emotional development, as well as his or her relationships in the learning environment, don't. The trouble is, any damage is more damage than any child should go through, and that is why families and school staff must work together to help all without their being bullied.

I believe school administrators must actively work toward a no-tolerance policy on bullying. Teachers and other authority figures cannot continue to turn a blind eye and just go on with their lessons. Most important, parents and siblings should be proactive in not only being role models but also being loving, observant confidants.

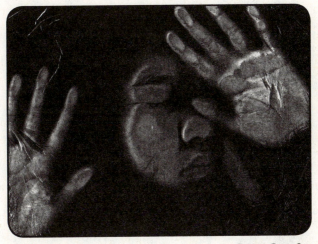

© 2013 Carrie Sun

Gayboy

Andrew Ramos

I am the victim. Shameful experiences race through my memory. Names like "gaylord," "gayboy," and "high-voice" jabbed me emotionally, just like those who sneered at me.

Throughout school, I have been called "gay" because of my higher-than-average voice. I remember walking through the halls of middle school and noticing kids glancing at me and then grinning at their friends, an unspoken joke at my expense passing with their looks. I remember the dread dragging down my heart and an uncomfortable sensation creeping up my back. My classmates would call me names like "gayboy" to my discomfort. These experiences always ended with me, red-faced with my head down, quickly shuffling away.

At that age, I saw being called "gay" as a curse and thought I was not normal. Any time people gathered for school events, anxiety filled my veins in fear that I would be called names. All it took was one catalyst, and waves of accomplices would begin pointing and whispering, "Look, it's the gay kid." Being singled out was common.

I was an outsider. Both boys and girls would flee when I approached—they didn't want to be called "friend of gayboy." And so I became the lonely, misunderstood Gay Kid. This title would graduate with me to high school, where, fortunately, such overt confrontations were less common.

After thinking about these painful experiences and analyzing who I am now, I realize a few things about my tainted age of innocence. I know that it's not these small occurrences that shape a life—it's the individual who decides how his life will be shaped. If I allow the name-calling and bullying to anger or depress me, it is my fault. If, however, I ignore it and carry on enjoying my life and the world around me, I am taking control of my life.

Allowing petty, ignorant acts to dominate your mind is unproductive. I have learned to have priorities and goals and to set my mind to more important things, including my future. However, I realize that these experiences have helped make me the person I am today, and I am very proud of who I am.

Kids, Meet the Real World

Elizabeth Ditty

Every month my school's principal selects a handful of students to take part in a student advisory committee meeting. Often, teachers and other faculty members attend. The topic of a recent meeting really hit home for me: school bullying.

When the topic was introduced, students immediately began to chime in with positive comments about our school's social climate. I was completely shocked. As they spoke, a fire began to build in my chest, and anger swelled in my heart. I took a breath and counted to ten. Looking around at the other students, I realized that they were all considered "popular."

I had been bullied for many years, but I hadn't been a victim at this school, although I had witnessed it happening every day. I had mostly interacted with kids on the lower end of the social ladder at my former school. Despite being tormented daily there, I have a happy, upbeat personality. My principal would probably be shocked to learn that I used to go home every day and cry because of the way I was treated by my peers.

At the meeting, the results of a schoolwide bullying survey were presented. Gasps and moans filled the room as the students on the committee disagreed with the negative results. I, on the other hand, wasn't a bit surprised.

The popular kids began to complain that the questions weren't written in a way students could understand. I watched as they tried to make excuses for the fact that bullying is everywhere in our school. The answers were in black and white in front of us, but they tried desperately to deny the facts.

As the discussion proceeded, a cheerleader interjected, "This is the real world. Students need to learn how to deal with others!"

I took issue with her comment. Bullying isn't a normal part of the real world. Humans are expected to treat one another with respect. School should not be an exception. It should not be a place where it's okay for a student to yell, "Hey, you fat whale, how about a Twinkie?" It should not be a place where young people are driven to suicide because of the emotionally and physically hurtful acts of others.

© 2013 Michelle Moy

Suicide from bullying is on the rise in young people, but have you ever heard of an adult committing suicide over harassment at work? If someone were to call a coworker a "fat whale," they would be fired or at least face serious discipline. Why isn't this true in our schools? Bullying prevention should receive at least as much attention and enforcement in schools as a ban on cell phones, but, sadly, it doesn't.

During high school, students should be preparing for the "real world" by learning to accept differences and treat others with respect. Teachers should be observing students as they interact in the halls, and those who bully should be reprimanded. A bully who isn't taught that his actions are wrong will enter the real world woefully unprepared to interact professionally and respectfully with others.

If My Pillow Could Speak

Claire Davis

If my pillow could speak,
The things it would say,
Being crushed to my chest
And cried into each day.
It would talk of the stains
That marked its soft linen,
The tears that had made them,
The state that I've been in.

It'd recall all the stories
I'd mumbled and sighed
Of insults and sneers
Heard at school
And online.

It would tell of the sadness,
Inform of the pain,
And how I had been shattered—
Again
And again.

It'd share my true anguish
And my mask, worn to hide it.

The want
To
Give
In,
The endeavor to fight it.

I'm sure it would wonder
Why so many are meek;
It would say,
"Stand up . . ."
If my pillow could speak.

Chapter Three

STANDING UP

*"We shall never know all the good
that a simple smile can do."*

—Mother Teresa

Take a Joke, Sweetheart

Jessica C. Rockeman

He leans over my desk, his body casting a shadow over my writing. Two fists are suddenly pressed hard next to my book, giving him an undeserved air of authority.

"You know they're just joking, right?"

His voice is gentle, as if he's speaking to a timid animal, but his stance is meant to intimidate.

I nod slowly, confused, as my blood boils. "I'm aware that they're joking, but the jokes offend me," I say.

He takes a deep breath, a nearly undetectable smile playing at the corners of his lips. He shoves his sleeves up. "The more you ask them to stop, the more they'll just keep doing it. That's how they work." He's telling me what many have tried to explain before: boys don't change, boys don't stop, boys won't listen to you, boys will be boys.

And oh, he is so smart, his words so very wise. I know he thinks he is imparting some kindhearted wisdom. He's giving a helpful tip to the silly girl who's making a fool of herself by refusing to tolerate behavior that makes her and other girls uncomfortable. He's playing big brother, daddy, the savior on a white horse sent to shut me up.

I look at him, anger burning the back of my neck and cheeks. "So, because they won't stop, I should just shut up and deal? I should let them make sexist jokes that upset me?" We're in history class. I thought school was supposed to be a safe environment.

His smirk falters a bit. "They're just joking. They don't really mean it."

People are watching us; I can feel their eyes. I'm suddenly vulnerable. I want them to stop staring, to go away. I want this boy to sit down and stop towering over me.

"If they think those jokes are harmless, they're ignorant," I say. "Believe me, the jokes don't end with 'Women should stay in the kitchen.' They continue until they become sexual and even more inappropriate. I want them to stop now, before they go that far." I've seen it happen before, too many times.

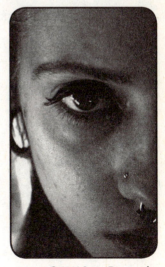

"I think you should just give it up before they gang up on you," he replies calmly, like an adult placating a cranky child.

I'm so upset I want to cry, but the steam gathering behind my eyes keeps the tears at bay. Who does he think he is, standing over me, a girl he's never spoken to before, telling me that my words are useless? That I might try to stand up for my sex, but

© 2013 Janna Dimopoulos

I'll always fail. If we were friends, I might have listened; if he'd spoken to me as a peer, I would have cared. But he's just pushing me down, stuffing me into a box to suffocate my useless, foolish words.

Ten minutes earlier, a group of boys had been trading sexist jokes about women. I had turned around in my chair and calmly said, "Please stop, for me. I'm asking you to stop." The boys looked doubtful, but they stopped, and I resumed my work. I didn't yell, lecture, or swear. I simply asked. I used words, the only weapon I know how to use, and everything was okay.

Now this boy has the nerve to try to tell me that my words don't mean anything. He's trying to take away my only defense. And he has no idea that he's being even ruder and more disrespectful than the ones who told the jokes in the first place.

But he doesn't have the power to shut me up. I will never stop fighting for what I believe is right. I will never stop standing up for myself, my friends, and my gender, and I will never stop using my (stupid, useless, fruitless, beautiful, powerful, amazing) words.

Finally he backs away, easing off my desk. Frustration shows on his face, even though he keeps his face stony and emotionless. "You'll never get anywhere with them, believe me. Don't say I didn't warn you," he says.

I didn't believe him.

Since that day, I have repeatedly spoken up to make others rethink their actions. Sometimes I fail and they don't stop. Sometimes my words get me into trouble. But sometimes I get through to them and even make a new ally.

Little did that boy know, he didn't break me down. He made me stronger.

How Are You?

Gemma Hahn

The children did not give a reason.

Maybe it was because I wore itchy, homemade sweaters that made me look like a fat ball of wool. Or maybe it was my terrible haircut, which made me resemble a Lego minidoll. Or maybe it was because I was quiet and overweight.

Whatever the reason, I was always the one picked last in gym class. I was the one who changed in the bathroom stalls so the girls wouldn't giggle about my chubby thighs and ugly birthmark. I was the one who scrubbed my body raw every morning to convince myself that I didn't smell, even if my peers groaned and held their noses when I stepped into the classroom.

But what I found even more unbearable than the taunting, pushing, cursing, and pointing was the feeling of cold air swirling in the empty seat next to me. It was the feeling of changing alone in the bathroom that got me, the distant titters of the girls in the changing room across the hall. It was a feeling that haunted me, that settled in my heart like a layer of frost, like the bitter aftertaste of unsweetened chocolate.

My parents knew what I was going through, and they tried to help me in their own ways. Mom would come to school with chocolate mint cupcakes or peanut butter cookies to share with the class. She knew her visits were not very successful—my class-mates only talked to me on that day and went back to bullying or ignoring me the next—but she kept trying, her smile weaken-ing little by little as the years passed. I always felt anxious and uncomfortable on those mornings, drowning in the sickeningly sweet scent of frosting and butter in our little car, because I felt guilty that I couldn't make friends despite Mom's efforts.

Dad's approach was to teach me to be strong, which I hated even more. "Hold your head high" was the common order he gave during all my years in elementary school, along with "Keep your chin up" and "Don't look away when people stare at you." He always held my hand when he said this, grip firm and almost bruising, and I would cry in my room afterward, not because my hand hurt, but because I was frustrated. I thought I could never be strong. I would always be the ugly duckling of my class, with-out the courage to look my peers in the eye.

Day by day, I became less confident, less communicative. My parents continued to encourage me to talk to others, had discus-sions with my teachers, and even enrolled me in counseling. Yet their efforts only discouraged me, because nothing ever seemed to change.

"You can only change things if you speak your mind," my counselor told me once. "It's not that hard. You can do it."

I just stared at her; I didn't have the heart to tell her that I could not.

But then there came a time when things did change.

It was my eleventh birthday, and I was alone in my room, eating cake. My door was locked because I had just yelled at my mom for persistently asking why I was not having a birthday party, even though she knew the reason. I was busy daydreaming about what would happen if I disappeared—how my parents would react, how sorry my mom would be for making me upset—when my dad knocked on the door.

I opened it a crack, expecting that he was going to reprimand me for being rude to Mom. Instead, he passed me the phone, explaining that it was Grandpa.

It had been a long time since I had spoken to Grandpa, since he lived in Korea and was too old and tired to visit. I pressed the phone to my ear and said hello. Grandpa greeted me with his soft laugh. Then he asked, "How are you?"

Three simple words that people say all the time. But they struck me so hard right in the middle of my chest that I couldn't breathe. I remained silent for a few seconds, savoring the warmth of my grandfather's words and the concern and caring behind his calm tone.

And that was when I came face to face with the fact that people love me. It was a fact that I had always thought but never realized. Although some of my classmates disliked me, there were still countless people who loved me with all their hearts. I was loved, I was precious, and I deserved better. There was no reason

I had to walk around school drenched in feelings of worthlessness and anxiety, to take the abuse passively. I needed to do what my counselor had always told me—I had to speak up.

And I got my chance the next day.

It was during class break, and some boys were tossing a basketball in the classroom. At one point, the ball hit me in the head, sending my glasses flying.

There was a short silence as the boys stared at me, wondering how I would react. Then one of them started to laugh, and the others uneasily joined in. They commented that if I weren't so fat, the ball wouldn't have hit me. Then they went back to their game, as if nothing had happened.

I stared at the boys, gently pressing my forehead. It hurt, almost to the point that it brought tears to my eyes.

I stood up suddenly, and my chair fell to the floor with a loud clatter. Some of my classmates jumped. I looked at the boys and pointed to my glasses on the floor.

"Pick them up," I said.

Everyone stared. I waited quietly, expecting the boys to laugh or yell. They did not. Mumbling something under his breath, the boy who hit me slowly trudged over and picked up my glasses. He came back with them and looked at me straight in the eye.

I didn't look away.

Quietly, the boy handed me the glasses and walked away, looking almost sorry. That was all that happened that day.

My life didn't change suddenly, like in a movie. I was largely ignored, and some peers continued to call me names and jostle me out of their way. But as the weeks passed and I found more opportunities to speak out against the unfairness, my bullies became quieter and quieter.

During that time I received a secret note, slipped between the pages of my textbook. It was anonymous, written on a green Post-It, asking if I wanted to have ice cream after school.

I looked around nervously, excited at the possibility of finally making a friend, but wary that the letter might be a joke. Then I noticed that a girl was watching me from across the room. She smiled shyly, and I smiled back. After school, we went to her house and stained our tongues red with popsicles. The next week, she asked me to join her dance class, where I met other girls. With some effort, I fought against my shyness and initiated conversations. And just like that, I made friends.

From then on, I didn't eat lunch alone. I didn't have to listen to the mean girls whisper behind my back, because my friends would tell them to stop. I continued to make friends, and within a few months, I felt as if I had always been confident, bright, and loved. It was amazing how quickly the change happened, how three simple words turned my life around.

Even now, in high school, I think of those times whenever I am faced with challenges. I remember the feelings of loneliness that followed me in elementary school, the years I believed I was being bullied because something was wrong with me, and how all it took was a little confidence to break down the barrier around me.

I think of my grandfather and of what a privilege it is to have people who love me, who would do anything to make me happy, whether baking cupcakes and offering advice or simply giving me a call.

I want others who are bullied to know this too. No matter how worthless some may make you feel, you are valuable to many others. And anytime I get the opportunity, I ask my loved ones, with all my heart, the simple question that changed my life:

"How are you?"

Singing His Praise

Milan Thakkar

Last year, our school's a cappella group decided that we would have student-run auditions to choose replacements for graduating seniors. It seemed like a democratic approach, but my first thought was that the auditions would become a popularity contest. Unfortunately, I was right.

This issue surfaced when Andrew, a freshman, auditioned. He was new to the area and had not received a warm welcome. He was socially awkward, which alienated him from peers and set him up for ridicule.

When our singing group heard that this "social outcast" was auditioning, many members approached me to insist that I not even consider him. I'm ashamed to say that I agreed. Why would we want a social outcast in our a cappella group? I laughed, agreeing every time.

But my resolve wavered when Andrew walked into the audition room and began to sing. He was by far the best we had heard. His range was greater, his tone richer, his pitch sharper than any of us. On merit alone, it was obvious that we should accept him. Still, I found myself influenced by the group, and my first vote placed him an undeserved fourth. Andrew managed to make it through that first round, though, which shocked me.

The second and final round of auditions proved Andrew to be undeniably worthy of a place in the group. Yet many of the girls still tried to keep him out, saying, "We'll be stuck with him for three whole years!"

My friend Peter urged me to join him in defending Andrew. At first I resisted, not wanting to make waves, but Peter persisted, arguing that Andrew's social status had nothing to do with his singing. He was right. Denying Andrew an invitation to the group would be a popular decision but morally wrong.

I'd never thought of myself as someone who blindly followed the crowd, but that conversation with Peter proved otherwise. I was horribly ashamed of myself. Peter was right: Andrew was not the issue. We were. Not choosing Andrew meant we opposed anyone different from us. His voice was unequivocally better than any of ours, but we were ready to throw him over simply because he didn't fit into our social system.

Peter must have spoken with other members too, because when the final votes came in, Andrew made the cut. I admire Peter's insight and leadership in making the group see Andrew as a talented individual worth accepting and getting to know.

I hope that one day I will find myself in another situation like that, so I can have the chance to make the right choice the first time, even if it isn't easy or popular.

Done Being a Victim

Brandi O'Donnell

I rushed to school on a crisp Monday morning. The grass was lined with frost, and my breath billowed visibly. As I approached the building, I mentally prepared myself for the daily onslaught of bullying. In the social strata of my high school, I was at the bottom.

Moving to a new town freshman year was tough. Even now, as a junior, the harassment continues. I am called fat or dyke, shoved, tripped, and even threatened. Even before I came out as a lesbian, students saw through my armor and attacked. I always wondered why these kids were so cruel. Didn't they realize that mistreating others could push them to the brink of suicide?

For many years, I had battled chronic depression. When I moved from my old town, I hoped that the bullying would stop. It didn't. My high school was separated into distinct cliques that hated each other. And beginning freshman year, it felt like they all hated me too, even though they knew nothing about me.

That Monday, I went home in tears after finding an anonymous note suggesting I should kill myself to stop the spread of my "gayness." The intolerance sickened me, and I finally decided I had to do something. I refused to keep my head down and be ridiculed anymore. If I didn't advocate for myself, no one else would.

I returned to school the next day with a feeling of strength, renewal, and pride. I walked with my head held high past the students who daily gave me dirty looks and taunts. A boy smirked as I passed.

"Hey, come back, nasty dyke!"

Enough was enough. I turned around, and with every ounce of self-respect I had, I glared at him. "You have no idea what words like that do to somebody, do you? You disgust me," I shot back. I walked away with a huge grin on my face. His face shone red with embarrassment at being told off.

I was shaking, my palms were sweaty, and I was sure my heart would beat out of my chest—but I was proud of myself. I had never stood up to anyone before, but it was time for a change. I was determined to destroy the vicious cycle that had been my life for too many years.

Every now and then I still get verbally harassed, but the bullying is not at the same level. The dirty looks continue, but I keep my head up and face my attackers with more confidence.

I no longer blame myself for being bullied. I am not a victim. No one should ever feel that they aren't worthy to stand up for themselves. No one is unlovable. You are worth it.

Some Say Good, I Say Pain

Natalie Rivera

Some say good
That you get bullied
Because you bullied me.
But I say pain,
Which is what I feel
When I see you get hurt.

Even though you
Did me wrong,
Does that mean
That I should delight
In another's misery?

No, because
When I was at the bottom,
I didn't want
The bystanders to join in
The bullying.
I wanted them to be
My voice when you had
Taken it away.

So I won't be a bystander,
I'll be the one to help you up.
Some say good,
I say pain.

Turn Around

Bridgette Rainey

Bullies seem to be everywhere. They prowl the school halls and sometimes even our homes. They break down the weak and rip others apart to feed their black souls.

It was freshman year when I met Jeff in our overcrowded cafeteria. It wasn't the most pleasant first encounter. But it was one that neither of us will ever forget. His rudeness and hurtful words led to an interaction that may have changed his perspective—and his reputation—for the better.

There is a boy named Nathan, who is autistic. On the first day of school, my friends and I noticed him wandering from table to table, waiting for someone to invite him. So I asked him over, and he has sat with us ever since. Nathan takes special education classes—ironically enough, with Jeff.

The day I met Jeff, I could sense something was different with Nathan. As Jeff confidently approached our table, Nathan refused to look at him, and I quickly realized why.

"Nathan, you're fucking retarded," Jeff blurted out in front of everyone.

Before he even finished this sentence, I was out of my seat. I whipped around and looked Jeff in the eyes.

"Did you honestly just say that?" I fumed. "Who do you think you are treating a classmate that way? Does it make you feel better about yourself to call him names? You need to turn around, walk away, and never speak to Nathan like that again." Then I added one of those mom-like statements to make sure he got the point. "Understand?"

It is now the end of my sophomore year, and Nathan still sits at my lunch table. Not only has Jeff never returned to our table, but his discipline referrals have decreased by half since last year, and he was chosen by his teachers as the most improved student. As much as I wish my actions were the main reason for Jeff's turnaround, I don't believe my few sentences were entirely responsible for his changed ways. But I do know that Nathan felt important to at least one person that day.

© 2013 Anton Largaespada

Sometimes changing a bully is difficult and even impossible. But if you don't try, those who are bullied will never know how much you care, and those who bully will continue to think their actions are acceptable. You can choose to remain a silent bystander, or you can take a stand to defend others. It's up to you.

Enter Girl

Maggie Brooks

Girl enters school.
Girl walks to locker.
Girl sees bully.
Girl tries to hide, fails.
Girl goes home, crying, and kills herself.

I wish this scene were acted out on a stage, with the actress faking her fear, the tech guy sweating in the back as he moves the spotlight to point at her. The audience would sit in creaking seats, fanning themselves, passively watching. They would listen. They would stay silent. When the girl kills herself and the show is over, they would clap. But this is not a show. This is real life. This is bullying. Yet, like the audience, we remain silent.

I believe bullying comes from prejudice, fear, and social pressure. I cannot say there will be a day when people are impervious to society's expectations. But I do know that we have the capacity to speak out and help others.

The teen years are a particularly difficult and vulnerable time. Every change takes place as though we are onstage. Our bodies, our clothes, our gender identity, our friends, our opinions, our race are all on view, and all are under attack. In the process of discovering who we are, we are constantly being judged by others, and we feel the blows. Everyone feels it. Even bullies.

Bullying can't be fixed piecemeal. If you only help the victim, the bully will still have nowhere to go, no one to turn to. And if you focus on stopping the bully, you leave behind a person who has been broken and needs support to glue them back together. These characters' arcs are intertwined; what happens to one affects the other.

The audience watching knows the truth as the scene unfolds. They know they have witnessed bullying, have done it, or have let it happen.

Girl enters school.
Girl walks to lockers
Girl sees bully.
Friend in hall looks at girl, smiles.
Girl smiles back.
Girl survives.

Remember, this is real life. This isn't a show. You may be watching, but you are not just the audience. Don't stay silent. Speak.

Chapter Four

CELEBRATE DIVERSITY

*"In the sky, there is no distinction of
east and west; people create distinction
out of their own minds and then believe them."*

—*Buddha*

Thanks, Jacob

Lamisa Chowdhury

In the middle of a pep rally, while everyone was participating in some wildly ritualistic dance, I peered over at Jacob. He was clapping furiously, his greasy hair brushing his face chaotically. He was laughing loudly and stomping both feet with zeal. Then I noticed the girls next to him, whispering and pointing. At Jacob.

Jacob is immeasurably intelligent. His hair hangs haphazardly around his pale face. Sometimes it gets stuck in his glasses. Pimples dot his upper lip. When I think about him, I think of Charlie from *Flowers for Algernon*, because sometimes Jacob can be so smart it overwhelms others.

In the seventh grade, popular boys and girls would crowd around him, asking him to define simple words like "book." He would reply with highly intellectual language, almost incomprehensible to the other kids. They would ask him again and again until he became so exasperated he'd pound his fists on the table. Then they would laugh maniacally.

For our ninth-grade talent show, Jacob performed his own

song, a beautiful compendium of the periodic table. He wore a rainbow lab coat and moved his arms like a conductor. Students recorded his performance on their cell phones, and it went viral on Facebook, with commenters saying all kinds of mean things. I don't like to think about why this happened.

When I think about people making others feel so, so small, my blood churns in my veins. My voice fragments into shards of poisoned glass with rage and anguish. It feels like someone has dipped a blade in acetone and forced it down my throat.

We should all aspire to be like Jacob, to display our passions and enthusiasm publicly, arranged like mosaic tiles for all to see. What Jacob did was magnificent. During a stage when most teens cling to each other, craving conformity, Jacob was true to himself.

Jacob helped me understand diversity. It means sharing your life with others without being ashamed. It means being willing to let others learn from your life. It means being okay with vulnerability for the sake of human connectedness. Being honest is the biggest risk you can take in this world. But it is the only way we can learn, grow, and mend our human community.

So guess what? I'm legally blind in my left eye. I hate jeans. I have acne on my back. I think astrology is baloney. I wash my hair every third day. I can't wait to take anatomy and cut into a corpse. I'm a Muslim, but I feel far away from God. I'm not ashamed to tell you that my parents hail from an impoverished country. I cry like it's my religion. Sometimes I only eat food cold.

We are all as beautifully strange as Jacob.

Love Thy Neighbor, Except for Some

Shreekari Tadepalli

We live in a media-saturated world. Skim the paper, and the debate rages over questions of race with cases like Trayvon Martin. Turn on the television, and our political leaders are discussing the healthcare rights of women versus men. Open a web page and Lady Gaga, Chris Colfer, and other celebrities are banding together to fight homophobia. As a nation, we're finally starting to take a stand and fight the hate.

As an Indian-American daughter of immigrants, the worst discrimination I've faced hasn't been about skin color, gender, or sexual orientation. With these, if a situation truly got out of hand, I could always turn to an authority figure for support—after all, racism, sexism, and homophobia are popular issues now, and resources are seconds away.

But another form of hatred and prejudice persists. A silent menace sweeps our nation, appearing in subtle ways through innocuous words like "service" and "unity." Sometimes it's a friend's simple statement—persistent, nagging, trying to drive a point home. Sometimes it's nothing more than a tone of voice, an air of superiority within a clique from which I am expressly forbidden. And then, sometimes, it's not so subtle—a comment on Facebook that devolves into a fiery thread of anger, ego, and hate speech. An accusation leveled at a group of people, left to defend an identity that they never saw as flawed.

You see, I am not part of the Christian majority.

Though our Constitution provides for freedom of religion, the First Amendment also shelters those who seek to change others' beliefs. Their right to free speech allows my classmates to tell me to go to church with them, to find Jesus, because the path I follow—my religion of Hinduism—is wrong. The school administration punishes my peers for saying the n-word or for calling someone a faggot. But they're at a loss when my classmate tells me that I pray to clay pots and am going to hell, or when another student asks if I'll come back from India kowtowing to cows.

As we seek to educate teenagers about racism, sexism, and homophobia in an effort to combat bullying, we have failed to address the issue of religious elitism. Somewhere amidst the school-sponsored Bible study and prayer groups, students are taught that pressuring someone to convert is acceptable. When I'm told that as a non-Christian I have no place in America, it isn't just me that the bullying hurts.

Maintaining religious freedom is important, and so is learning to understand others' beliefs, especially when they differ from our own. The embodiment of this acceptance is found in Christianity: "Love thy neighbor as thyself" leaves no room for religious superiority or exclusivity.

The Orange Bracelet

David Chrzanowski

People tell me it's weird that I wear a bracelet a homosexual gave me. When I started wearing it, I found myself having to answer questions about my sexual orientation. When I'm asked about it, I laugh or say, "You're right—it's dumb," but that's not how I really feel.

My family has always been very accepting. Coming from this open-minded environment, I got quite a shock when I started high school. My overprivileged, conservative, Wonder Bread, Southern community held prayer groups preaching death to gays, and teachers turned a blind eye to peer abuse. Worst of all, this behavior was treated as normal.

When I became a drum major, I attended a camp for drum majors from across the country. There, I saw that most marching bands serve as a refuge for school misfits, those brave few who dare to be themselves. Oddly, my own Pleasantville-style band didn't fit this stereotype.

Just when I thought I was leading an army of suburban clones, an "unconventional" freshman named Austin joined the band.

He was a flautist, and a darned good one. With spiky blond hair, clear-polished toenails, and pink designer glasses, he was very open in his sexual orientation. He stood out in another way too: not once did he do anything with the intention of being offensive. He was never self-righteous, defensive, or overbearing. He must have known that people talked behind his back, yet he never showed any bad feelings. In a world of disgusting conformity, I found myself admiring the most detested person I knew.

Austin surprised me on our band trip to Disney World by offering me a gift: an orange leather bracelet that he'd made, inscribed with "Drum Major" on one side. The presentation was bold, fearless. Members of the band were everywhere, watching in horror, confused and judging.

I wear that bracelet every day. But not because I am gay or because I particularly like orange. I wear it because it's more than a bracelet to me. It's my way of

© 2013 Jessica Padilla

declaring that Austin does not stand alone against the tide of fear-laced conformity. By wearing it, I silently profess to all who witnessed our exchange that a failure to understand something should not lead to its persecution. Every day I put on the orange bracelet as a reminder of the excellent example Austin has set for us all.

The Smallest Star

Summer Davis

Sticks and stones
Will break my bones,
And words
Will break my heart.

I've been beaten,
I've been slapped,
I've been stepped on,
And nobody
Turned around.

My face has been
Cut by words.
My arms
Tattooed with names.
My stomach is branded
With hate.

And my legs . . .
Well,
My legs are bruised
From all the falls
Where no one
Would catch me.

My own thoughts
Are drowned out
By the remarks
Of others.

I'm the smallest
Star in the night's sky.
My only reason
For being is
To make the
Brighter stars look better.
This is how they view me.

But I know
That I matter.
I am a small star,
But my light
Burns longer than theirs.
I am more than
A raindrop in the Pacific.

I am a storm cloud
Pouring down on the earth
To spread life-giving water.
I do matter.
Others can boast,
But I don't have to listen.

I am me.
No reason to change.

They talk about me
To heal their own hurt.
There is no reason to hate them
For hating me
Because it doesn't matter
What they think.
Just because they
Don't like me
Doesn't mean that
I can't love myself.

I can deal with the
Cuts
Tattoos
Brands
And bruises,
Because I love
Who I am.

Uncivil Discourse

Altay Sedat Otun

There is an unspoken and controversial truth that needs to be addressed: every individual who's a minority is the target of bullying in the United States at some point. It's as simple as that.

Unfortunately, the majority of Americans are unaware of the bullying that goes on around them because they don't see that not all bullying is as obvious as one student beating up another.

Some acts of bullying are broadcast nationally, like when a gay soldier was booed at the 2012 Republican presidential primary debate. Some are more subtle, like Muslims being targeted for searches at airports. Every day, some minority is the target of discrimination.

I notice both the subtle and obvious acts of bullying because I have been a target myself. Being a teen isn't easy, but growing up as a gay male from a Muslim family in the post-9/11 South only makes it harder.

I am a bully's dream.

According to research by the Southern Poverty Law Center, hate crimes against the LGBT and Muslim communities are on the rise.

Because of my religion, I was bullied by kids who were taught by their parents and the media that every Muslim harbors a vendetta against the West. Kids who were taught that gays have a deep-seated obsession for straight boys bullied me because they were afraid I would come on to them. And the kids who were taught to hate both Muslims and gays simply could not get enough of me.

I was called awful names and racial slurs. My locker was vandalized and my e-mail account was inundated with hate mail. The bullying I experienced is not unique in any way. But it is an experience that I hope will one day become a rarity in our society. And so we must understand what causes verbal or physical abuse against minorities.

I believe it is the subtle forms of bullying that empower people to commit hate crimes. When a congressman openly champions anti-immigration legislation, it encourages citizens to act out against these groups. When presidential candidates make hateful comments against the LGBT community, it fuels ignorant individuals to commit violence or discriminate against gay, lesbian, bisexual, and transgender Americans.

© 2013 Shaughnelene Smith

My point is simple: if we want to end bullying, we must first bring back a sense of civility to our national discourse. Setting large-scale examples of tolerance and inclusion will provide a better model for promoting understanding and acceptance between individuals.

The Christmas Tree

Ashley E.

I live in a small town where everyone knows everyone else. There used to be a large Jewish community, but it has declined over the years. In seventh grade, I found out that people were calling me names behind my back—names I'd never heard before that had to do with my being Jewish. I remember crying for the first time in front of my classmates when I found out what they meant. Even though I begged my teacher to let me go to the guidance counselor, he refused.

In my middle school, the higher your grades, the more respected you were. Although I was an honors student, the boy who started the bullying was class president and got even higher grades. No one I told would believe that he had anything to do with bullying.

Finally, I confided in my neighbor, a Board of Education member, who helped me take action. I thought my bullies would finally get what they deserved, but again I was wrong. My principal let that boy off with a warning and forced another girl to write me an apology I knew she didn't mean. I couldn't believe I had suffered so much and this was all the retribution I got. I felt I couldn't trust anyone, especially adults.

In eighth grade, I was unpopular because everyone believed I was making too big a deal of the situation. People would pretend to sneeze "A-Jew" whenever they passed me, shoved me on the stairs, and made fun of how I dressed.

I kept telling myself that they were jealous because I was smarter and better off. I decided not to report the harassment, since nothing had been done in the past. And I had lost hope.

One day I was called to the office. My favorite teacher had told the principal about what I was facing. He had heard kids bullying me and felt it was time to take action. Finally, the principal was forced to react. Three girls were expelled, and I got back everything I felt I had lost: my confidence, trust in authority, and hope.

School did not get better, though. My peers blamed me for the girls' expulsion, but I didn't feel bad for a second. They had brought it on themselves.

I started high school thinking the bullying was finally over, but I still heard anti-Semitic slurs in the hallways. One night, I was home studying when the doorbell rang. I heard my grandmother yelling and looked out the window. Someone had put a Christmas tree in our front yard. I pretended to laugh it off, not showing how much it bothered me.

Two weeks later, a boy who had gone to my school told me he wished he could "slap some Christian" into me and that he and some other boys were responsible for the tree. Once again, I felt like I didn't care. Apparently those boys had an obsession with trying to make me miserable, and I finally understood that it was their problem. Not mine.

Prejudice is a part of life, but with experience comes wisdom, and in the three years I have had to deal with this hate, I've learned a lot about how to persevere.

The R-Word

Lily Houghton

"I'm gonna call him retarded!"

This was the first time I ever really got mad at my brother. He was talking about a kid who bullied him at school. In his mind, name-calling was the best way to get back at the bully. Hearing him say this made me really sad.

My brother is autistic and goes to a special school. Even in an environment surrounded by kids like him, where he's supposed to fit in and feel accepted, he is being bullied and learning to bully others.

Personally, I have never been badly bullied. I seemed to have flown just under the radar. Occasionally someone would call me a name, or say I looked like a boy because of my short hair, but that never really hurt me. I thought I had escaped the horror stories I'd heard and didn't really believe that bullying could be as awful as it was portrayed in the movies.

Then I started spending more time with my brother.

Henry is sweet, well-rounded, and polite. He's also delightfully unique. He has memorized the number of every taxicab we've ever been in, knows all the subway lines by heart, and swears he can never get lost. I used to believe him, until I saw how lost he was in understanding his peers.

Other kids would call Henry names or tell him to shut up. But the worst was when Henry thought someone was his friend, but they were just using him for a laugh. He would dance when the other kids asked him to, sing Justin Bieber songs for their entertainment, and trip and fall on purpose just to see them laugh. Henry thought they were laughing because he was funny. He thought he finally had friends. But instead, as soon as Henry would leave the room, the bullies would talk about what an idiot they thought he was. My brother became a clown for kids he thought were his friends.

Henry thought he was part of the group, and so he thought he could use words like "retard" to describe other kids. When he said that word, it hurt me more than he knew. I told him why it is never okay to call anyone retarded, or any names, but I couldn't bring myself to tell him his "friends" were actually bullying him.

If you have ever called a special-needs student "retarded" or used the word to joke with your friends, I hope you'll remember my story. Even if the victim doesn't understand what you mean, certainly there are better ways to get a laugh than at another's expense.

And It Keeps Swinging
Julie Block

Gay. Fag. Queer.
Gay. Fag. Queer.
The chair in the corner of the room
It smiles at me.
It laughs at me.
Every time I see it, it reminds me.

Gay. Fag. Queer.
The tiles in the ceiling
They look down on me.
They pity me.
Every time I see them, they remind me.

Gay. Fag. Queer.
The 6'3" monster who tore my world apart,
He doesn't see me anymore.
He's gone.
But his memory still reminds me.

Gay. Fag. Queer.
The rope is still there, too.
It just stares at me.
It still feels heavy, carrying too much weight.
It swings, back and forth.
Gay. Fag. Queer.
Gay. Fag. Queer.

Back and forth.

Back and forth.

He was so young, so innocent

And he knew what he wanted to be

When he grew up.

But he will never get there.

Gay. Fag. Queer.

Gay. Fag. Queer.

Back and forth.

Back and forth.

What is so wrong with knowing what you want?

With being who you are?

With loving who you want to love?

Gay. Fag. Queer.

Back and forth.

I would blame it all on him,

On the monster,

But everyone else who watched

Who laughed

Who stared, dumbfounded,

And did nothing.

I blame them, too.

Gay. Fag. Queer.

Back and forth.

It never stops.

And it never will.

Silent No More

James Sares

"Is he gay?"

"I think so."

"Yeah, I'm pretty sure."

"Ask him."

"Hey, are you—"

The bell cut off the cacophony of gossip. There had always been rumors about my sexual orientation, but the painfully straightforward questions made me cringe. My ears burned with anger and embarrassment as I walked away as fast as I could, feeling awkward. I tried to shrug off the girls' malice as ignorance, but my blood rose as I heard their laughter follow me.

My high school was about as homogenous and conservative as it gets in a "liberal" state like Massachusetts. Diversity seemed thousands of miles away, and any form of social deviation was grounds for ostracizing and bullying. Same-sex marriage was legalized in Massachusetts in 2004, on my birthday, which provided another point for mocking and did little to improve things for students like me. I felt a great sense of disconnect between the "progress" of the gay rights movement and the conditions against which I, as a gay teen being bullied, struggled daily.

For the first couple years of high school, I got along by keeping my mouth shut, enduring the taunting, and burying myself in schoolwork. I made tenuous friendships as a nomad between social groups, never getting too close. Still, I had no language to describe the oppression I was experiencing, so the feelings burned inside of me, repressed as internalized homophobia, until they overflowed into anger.

I remember one day in the auditorium, overhearing the abusive whispering of my peers, I could no longer contain my feelings. I turned around and shouted, "You people are so rude!" Even that small act of defiance, that microrefusal of oppression, was met with one word that shut me down again: *Faggot.*

For all the bullying I had endured, that word, that time, was sneered with such viciousness that it physically took me aback. I will never forget the cutting feeling in my chest. That word reduced me to a single concept and left a wound, carved time and again, that would take years to heal.

After weeks of agonizing, I promised myself that I would not be silenced again. Gradually, I came out to my closest friends, then my sister, and finally my parents. With their support, I grew more comfortable. My face no longer reddened at the mention of homosexuality, and instead of being embarrassed by intrusive questions, I proudly proclaimed, "Yes, I am gay."

As I gained confidence, I was finally able to face the ignorance and homophobia in my school. I spoke with authority, and people began to listen and respect me. They recognized that being gay did not mean being weak, and that I would not degrade myself with silence. I became a leader in my school, and during sophomore year, I joined the Gay-Straight Alliance. My participation helped me accept myself and forgive those girls and the others who hurt me with their ignorance.

I was fortunate to have never faced physical threats in high school, but I learned intimately how words shape our world and have very real consequences. Now, almost five years out of high school, I reflect on the effects of bullying that continue to haunt my daily life: I avoid crowds as I walk down the street, I distrust the motivations of strangers, and I keep myself on guard for any signal of male aggression.

Through campaigns like It Gets Better, which began several years after I left high school, we often hear stories of liberation through finding new community and career successes. Behind many of these accounts are themes of overcoming homophobia or transphobia by fleeing toward new people or places. Yet this possibility of movement is also a privilege. What about those who cannot escape their bullying? I want to tell them: bullying is not your fault, but it cannot be wished away or separated from your life experiences. Yet hate is unproductive. I've learned that I cannot hold grudges or become bitter; hate comes from fear and ignorance.

My experiences have helped me to better understand homophobic people and how to deal with them. I hope that through interacting with me and getting to know me, some of them will change their views about GLBTQ people.

Chapter Five

FRIEND OR FOE?

*"It takes a great deal of bravery
to stand up to our enemies, but just
as much to stand up to our friends."*

—J. K. Rowling

Cheyenne

Kaitlyn "Hope" Partin

Cheyenne is the most hated girl in school. Hypocrite. Wannabe. Loudmouth. Some of what they say about her is true, but most isn't. Not that it matters in junior high. If you're hated, you're hated. That's just the way it works. I can see eyes rolling as she passes. Even some of the teachers eye the classroom clock, counting every second she occupies their time. It's hard to watch. There are times when the way Cheyenne is treated makes me want to cry.

"Let's play basketball," says the cutest boy in school one day.

I groan along with every other girl in gym class. We shuffle toward the court as the boys line up under the basket.

"What's going on?" I call. "Aren't we playing basketball?"

"We are. We'll show you how it's done."

The game is simple. Every student takes a shot. If you miss, you go to the back of the line. If you make the shot, you choose any player to run a lap around the school field. If you keep making shots, your target keeps running laps.

Cool, I think. *It'll be fun to see who has to run, who makes the most shots, who strikes out.* Then I see Cheyenne. Her braids swing in front of me as we line up. I tense up and try not to think what might happen.

The jock takes his first shot. *Swish!* In goes the ball. He scans the line of nervous students then calls Cheyenne's name. I try to stay optimistic as she starts running. The jock misses his next shot and another student steps up. It's a cheerleader, and she takes aim just as Cheyenne gets back in line. I whisper a prayer that the girl will miss. As I open my eyes, I see her shot. Nothing but net.

"Cheyenne!" the cheerleader calls in a high, condescending voice. My heart sinks as the already sweat-soaked Cheyenne begins her second lap.

I try to comfort myself: the cheerleader and the jock are a couple. They must have planned this as a little joke. But even as I think this, I know I'm wrong. I watch in horror as every successful shot results in Cheyenne's name being called. As the boy in front of me sinks his shot, I watch the panting Cheyenne struggle back to the court.

Before he can say her name, I step out of line. "I'll run for her."

I don't wait for anyone's approval or permission. I just take off.

As I finish my first lap, I hear the whispers. "Cheyenne's making Kaitlyn run for her" and "Dorks shouldn't get special treatment."

I see Cheyenne's terrified face and know she can't defend herself. I grab her shaking hand and pull her into a jog beside me. She doesn't wait for me to speak. She doesn't have to. The tone of our conversation was set the moment I stepped out of line.

© 2013 Rebecca Brown

"I can run," she begins.

I nod and smile. "I know. I just thought you could use some company."

She cracks a smile but freezes as our eyes meet the rest of class. I shake my head and turn for another lap. Suddenly, as if this proved my trustworthiness, Cheyenne pours her struggles into my already ringing ears. I realize what she must go through every day. She briefly explains her strained home life and how school isn't even an escape for her.

I don't speak. I don't try to advise her. I don't tell her everything is going to be okay. She just needs someone to listen. I squeeze her hand, and we head back to join the rest of the class. As our dirty sneakers hit the pavement, I tap Cheyenne's shoulder.

"Dorks don't get special treatment. Friends do."

My Frenemy

Elana Burack

She's not a typical bully. But then again, I'm not a typical victim.

We were best friends all through middle school. We sat together in class, went to parties, shared secrets—normal stuff. But one September day, the good times came to a sudden end. I decided to sit with some other kids I liked at lunch, and apparently that wasn't allowed. She punished me for eating with them. She questioned who my friends were and whether I was loyal to her. But meanwhile, I caught her gossiping about me with another girl.

In order to feel better about herself, my friend wanted me to feel worse, and it worked. I became depressed and went through times of extremely low self-confidence. I didn't know what I wanted or who my friends really were. I was alone a lot and often stayed home from school. I cried almost every day. I concentrated on academics to keep my mind off my nonexistent social life. My insecurities caused me to become confused about who I was.

That's when I realized how unhealthy our friendship was. I saw how she had been controlling me for years. Without realizing it, I had let her.

Bullying by friends is insidious because it's so hard to recognize. Her manipulation was seamlessly integrated into our friendship. Bullying isn't always a fight over lunch money or jokes about someone's clothes. It can be as subtle as instructing (instead of asking) a friend to wait by the lockers, or criticizing her for sitting at a different lunch table. When you start to do things because someone is telling you to and not because you want to, there's a problem. These may seem like little things, but in reality, this kind of controlling can be damaging.

I had to redefine myself without her negative influence. And so I created a mantra to guide me: "Define yourself. Be yourself. Love yourself." I had to make myself over into someone I could love again. And I did. And I stood up to her.

I thought I had gotten her out of my life. But I was wrong. We're sophomores now, and she hasn't changed. We're not friends, but we have classes together. She often interrupts my conversations, trying to undermine me and beat me at everything. But it's different now. Her words don't have the power they did in eighth grade. They hardly skim my surface. They no longer control me.

I deserve more than to live in her shadow. I am a stronger person for standing up to her, and I have grown from this experience. I have found out who my true friends are and have realized the simple beauty of being myself. I love who I am, and I have nothing to prove—to her or to anyone.

I'm not playing her game anymore.

The Bullet

Kenzie Estep

My breathing was heavy, and everything was a blur. Another tear trickled down my face. I tried my hardest to keep my hands steady, to hold my iPod still. But it was growing harder by the second as I watched the horrific scene before me.

On FaceTime, I saw my best friend, Aaron, holding a bullet. He looked at peace as he stared at the bullet in his hand. He seemed mesmerized by this object that was so small, yet so deadly.

To him, it was a godsend. It was the promise of an escape from all the pain and suffering. To me, it was a gift from hell, poised and ready to take my friend. I relived every moment with him, knowing that those memories could soon be all I had left. I was overcome by pain and sorrow. Then I was overwhelmed by a wave of rage.

I was furious, furious because I knew he didn't get to this place by himself. Our classmates had pushed him with their endless torment, daily bullying, and humiliation. Over the weeks, they'd made Aaron feel worthless. They had convinced everyone at school that he was a weirdo, a freak to avoid at all costs. They had fueled gossip about him that would be hard for anyone to live down.

Aaron was bisexual, and they thought the whole world should know.

People started to look at him differently. They no longer saw him as the football jock the girls loved and the guys envied. His friends abandoned him, scared to be around him for fear of being tormented too. People who didn't know him began to refer to him as "that bisexual kid." He received nasty looks from almost everyone as he walked down the hallway, the whispers echoing around him.

He felt like no one loved him anymore, all because of something he couldn't change. They had finally pushed him to the edge. One more push and it would all be over.

"Please, get rid of that," I pleaded.

"Why? It gives me comfort. Having it with me . . . knowing that I can stop it all if I need to. I can't give that up," he replied sadly.

"I won't be able to sleep tonight knowing you're in danger. I need you to do this for me. I need you to stay alive for me . . . I need you," I managed to whisper through my sobs. "Please."

He must have seen the pain in my face because—with a sigh—he stood up and filled the sink with water.

As he dropped the bullet in, I could suddenly feel myself breathe again.

Becoming friends with Caroline brought out my strong side. She made me realize my passion for art and music. Without her, I probably would still be friends with those four girls, hiding my feelings while laughing on the outside. So, the next time you see your friends picking on someone, follow your conscience and stand up for that person. You never know—he or she could change your life.

© 2013 Maya Gouw

Finding Caroline

Jessica Martin

All through elementary school, I was one of those girls. You know, the snotty, mean, I'm-better-than-everyone type. But that was just on the outside. On the inside, it was a different story. I was friends with the "cool" group, and by making other kids feel bad, we felt superior. Anyone who didn't fit our definition of normal was a target for harassment. I went along with my friends because I was scared they'd turn on me next.

One day a new girl came to our school. Caroline was different in every sense of the word, proudly sporting neon pink leg warmers, a lime-green jumpsuit, and a denim hat. Her attire was certainly unique, and I thought it was interesting and cool compared to my standard jeans and T-shirt. My friends, on the other hand, were threatened by her boldness.

From the minute Caroline walked into the room, the comments began. "What does she think she's wearing?" She put her head down in shame. She was just being herself. I felt horrible, but if I stuck up for her, I'd be the next target, and I didn't feel strong enough to oppose them. So I just sat there, my insecurity getting the best of me, and missed an opportunity to do the right thing.

As the year continued, my friends continued to harass Caroline every day, but she always kept her emotions in check, taking their insults in stride. I respected her for that and wished I could be that strong. Never defending her, my guilt grew.

Life went on as it usually does, and school ended. Trips to the beach were planned, and the smell of hot dogs and hamburgers filled the air, completing the sweet aroma known as summertime. I hung out with my friends, but I felt unhappy and untrue to myself. They never knew, though, because they never took the time to notice, and I never told them.

Soon enough, school began. A new school, new people—I couldn't wait. I was excited, yet terrified at the same time. Arriving at homeroom, I scanned the room, and to my disbelief, I saw not one of my friends from my old school. I was relieved and scared. A room filled with new people was a bit overwhelming. I quickly found a seat.

"Hey," a voice said from my left. I looked over and saw it was Caroline.

"Hey," I replied shakily. I was a bit nervous, expecting a verbal beating for being so mean to her the previous year. Boy, was I wrong. She couldn't have been nicer. She asked if I was nervous about starting this new school and confessed that she too had the jitters. We compared our grueling schedules.

As it turned out, Caroline and I were in most of the same

classes. The more we talked, the more I discovered h[...] were. We both loved drawing and playing the guitar[...] to meet someone who was interested in discussing[...] other than boys. When the bell sounded, we kept on[...] headed to class together.

On the way, I was stopped by my old school frien[...]

"Hey, Jess," they said, looking Caroline up and d[...] are you doing with her?"

"We're going to class," I replied.

"Oh, so you're best friends now?" they asked with[...]

They walked away laughing. I didn't know wha[...] rushed to my class, leaving Caroline behind. *Now I'[...] the big joke with my friends*, I thought dejectedly.

"Are you okay?" Caroline asked, her voice filled w[...]

"Why are you being so nice?" I shot back, angry b[...] guilt. Caroline had been nothing but nice to me, a[...] seem to return the favor.

"Because I know you aren't like them," she replie[...]

I didn't know how to react. I just smiled. I felt so[...]

Caroline and I grew very close, and I made other[...] were cool in their own ways. My former friends, ho[...] have such luck. After that day in the hall, they m[...] prey, using every weapon in their arsenal to try to bre[...] But with my new friends to support me, I was able t[...] My old friends remained a tight-knit group, not exp[...] social sphere, causing them to miss out on lots of [...] at the new school.

My Friends, My Bullies

Emily C. Farrugia

I looked down at the words in the book, standing out black against the white page, their meaning ringing in my ears, black amidst all the white noise.

The book, *Dear Bully*, is a collection of authors writing about their experiences of being bullied. It might help give you strength. Or it might open your eyes like it did mine. In that book, one author described her bullies as acting just like my friends do.

The first thing I thought was, *My friends aren't bullies. They love me and trust me. They care about me.* But then I thought more about it.

I thought about the times I sat at another lunch table because I couldn't stand them whispering behind their hands right in front of me. I thought about the times I felt sick to my stomach when I approached them, because I knew they would carry on their conversation without acknowledging me. I thought about when I asked them to listen to me and they just changed the subject. About how they laughed off their cruelty, calling it "just teasing." And about how I was so scared of their "teasing" that I had anxiety attacks walking to school.

I thought about how I'd always believed that as long as I kept the real me hidden, I would be immune to their insults, because they weren't for the "real" me. I thought about how I was so scared of being vulnerable and alone that I wouldn't let myself love anyone. I brushed off those emotional "moments of weakness" so I would seem strong, with no cracks in my armor for them to hurt me with.

I was scared reading that book, because it made me realize those little voices hidden deep within me were right. My friends weren't really friends; they were bullies. Ignoring and singling someone out aren't part of any real friendship.

Although this realization has made me sad, it's also making me stronger. I know that one day I will have real friends, people I can trust with my secrets, not people who will turn my secrets against me or make me feel like I'm alone.

I'm different from the authors in that book, though. That book was a way for them to reflect on their pasts. But I'm living this right now, and every day I'm right back in it.

My train to escape bullying hasn't arrived yet. But one day I'll jump on that train, and as it speeds past my bullies, I'll look out the window and flip them off. Not yet, but one day. And that gives me hope. But for now, I'm still living it.

The Worst Thing About Bullying

Rachel Chevat

The worst thing about
Bullying
Wasn't the
Wrist-twisting—
It wasn't the midnight marks
Scattered across my arms
Reminding me constantly
Of my toothpick-boned body
Weeping over
Lost self-esteem.

The worst thing about
Bullying
Wasn't the
Bad name listing—
The tiny words that
Worked like piranhas
Swimming through sound waves
Straight into
The worst of my dreams.

No,
The worst thing about

Bullying
All occurred in this one scene
Looking in the mirror, seeing
Faded bullies leave their
Names on my skin,
Seeing hollowed-out
Stars
In my eyes that would glisten.
Suddenly,
A toxic epiphany was
In the room with me,
Pinching my eyes and
Pulling at ends.

The worst thing about
Bullying
Is that they
Were
My
"Friends."

Confessions of an Ex-Bully

Amy Norton

You would never guess that I was a bully. I wasn't fearless, impulsive, or hot-tempered. I had a happy family life and no apparent troubles. So how could I be a bully?

Everyone focuses on victims and bystanders. No one tells the story from the bully's perspective, so people don't think about what leads someone to become a bully. I'm sharing my story with the hope that others may avoid the traps I fell into and come to understand that seeing the bully's side of things is necessary.

The first fact people need to learn is that every bully starts as a victim, whether the victim of an abusive home life, a bad self-image, or another bully.

In fourth grade, I moved to a new neighborhood. I made a few friends I considered my social lifelines. Two months into our friendship, one of them pulled me aside at lunch.

"No offense," she said, "but we don't really want you to sit with us anymore. We don't want you to hear what we're talking about."

I learned later that she had done this to others too, but nobody had warned me. That's the thing about bullies; we thrive off others' silence. Lack of communication and isolation are keys to any successful attack. I tried to act like everything was okay, but I grew bitter and lonely.

In sixth grade, I was willing to do anything to be accepted. I quickly realized that in my school, bringing somebody else down made you look good, and gossiping made others want to talk to you. I never attacked anyone physically or teased them to their face. Bullies like me hurt others by spreading lies. Rarely do we bully face-to-face.

I started rumors, I gossiped, I backstabbed, I excluded girls, and no one ever questioned my hurtful words. You see, bullies don't do it alone; we would be nothing without the support of others. There's a little bully inside most of us, eager to contribute because "Thank God, they're not talking about me."

Then I went too far. I said horrible things about my best friend and soon found myself living my worst fear. Suddenly I didn't have any friends to back up my attacks, and no one wanted to hear anything I said. It was painful at the time, but if I hadn't been excluded, I wouldn't have understood how I had made others feel. I might still be a bully.

So how can you stop bullying? Don't be silent. Stand up to bullies. Ask the victim if a rumor is true, or tell her what's being said behind her back so she knows who her real friends are. Console the victim, listen, be kind. Above all, be a friend.

Dear Friend

Meia Geddes

Do you remember that day in middle school when I was all alone and you came up and introduced yourself and your friends? You kept talking to me. You laughed and joked with everyone, and I was amazed. I still am. How could you be so humbly confident?

Could you see that I was unhappy? I don't think so; I hid it well. I was never interested in obvious grief. Just silent sorrow. Back then did you know how silent unhappiness could affect a person? How it could twist a mind into thinking so many negative thoughts?

You are not a social butterfly, but the way you embrace everyone and let them open up to you is more beautiful than any butterfly I've ever seen. I'd never known anyone like you, so gently persistent. I will always remember that.

Do you remember that movie where one girl sits alone at a table and another girl sits with her to be kind? Everyone thought that it was unrealistic. Even I scoffed a little. But I always felt like that girl, with you coming and rescuing me.

Can you believe I'm crying? Maybe I've only now realized what you did for me. I wonder if I'll ever have the courage to give you this letter. You'd probably deny everything.

We've drifted apart, but that's because you helped me drift. You helped me find myself, and I have other friends now. I see classmates who remind me so much of the person I was—letting the negatives outnumber the positives. Maybe that's why we are drawn to each other.

I want to be like you, my friend. I want to see the beauty in people and help them find it in themselves, the way you did for me.

Your grateful friend,

Meia

Attack of the Mean Girls

Lena Rawley

Teenage girls have the self-entitlement of celebrity heiresses and the aggression of Roman gladiators. Like vampires, they feed off the blood of the weak. They're pubescent monsters. Adolescent boogeymen.

With the determination of private assassins, when teenage girls find a target, they will stop at nothing to take it down. They're relentless. They're cruel. Their methods are insane. They should never be underestimated.

While my observations may be coming from a point of bias, that doesn't mean they are inaccurate. As a teenage girl, I think I know the type quite well. Not only am I a former mean girl myself, but I was also tortured, tormented, isolated, and socially maimed by them.

In middle school, I made the mistake of underestimating these skinny jean-clad monsters. Because I was one of them, I thought myself impervious to their cruelty. I watched them do unto others as they would later do unto me, and I felt no fear.

I was a fool, however, because teenage girls pick their targets by familiarity. They are just as likely to torment someone small and insignificant as they are to viciously turn on a friend. They identify the weakest link in their group, the prey that's easy for them to take down.

I was the weakest link. I was the wounded gazelle. And so I became their target.

It was eerie because when my demise began, I had no idea what was happening. Yes, it was slightly fishy that my "friends" stopped calling me, stopped saying hi in the hallway, but I assumed it was nothing.

© 2013 Abby Weeden

Again, I was wrong.

After the period of silence, all hell broke loose. They spread vicious rumors about me and threw dirty looks and foul words my way. I was forced from the lunch table and into social isolation.

Exactly a week after my isolation began, I received an e-mail from the ringleader of the group. The headline bluntly stated, "Fifty Reasons Why We Can't Be Friends with You." Underneath, as promised, were fifty reasons for my ostracism, ranging from my physical characteristics to my personality to my clothes.

I felt sick.

But I wasn't going to let them get me. Those hyenas didn't deserve my tears. I deleted the venomous e-mail, picked up the pieces of my self-esteem, and moved on. Over time, I found friends who were kind and accepting. Friends who wouldn't devour their own.

My experience, while obviously not ideal, is something I would not change. I don't see it as a stain upon the fabric of my life but more like an embellishment. It's a decorative brooch I wear with pride, a medal that says I overcame bullying, and so can you.

A Walk on the Wild Side

Kathryn Ferentchak

I am no bully. I am the type who gets uncomfortable when mere venting takes a vindictive turn. I am a bystander. I zip my lips and tell myself everyone has a right to their opinion.

But then again, they don't.

Off-campus privileges are the best. Of course, I am too cheap to pay for food and always pack a lunch, but taking a drive is a great way for people to bond. Unless you're riding with that kid who wants to show off his new mega-subwoofer, you are basically forced into conversation with your fellow passengers.

Coed cars are better than girls-only. Without the opposite sex, the claws come out. It becomes a matter of balance and gentle bids for superiority. This is when we start slamming people. "I hate . . . school . . . science teachers . . . ACTs and SATs . . . PDA . . . slutty girls." Suddenly subtopics are introduced. "She slept with who? . . . At that party they did what? . . . Her boyfriend doesn't know? . . . He cheats on her . . . They hooked up."

Then maybe someone will break the flow. Make a confession of her own. Reveal a dirty little secret just like those under fire.

Then the conversation stops. It is so uncomfortable.

I am a bystander. The innocent ones, the pure girls (or prudes, depending on your perspective) are actually the worst. You don't have to be "experienced" to be a bitch. They get rolling:

"Why would anyone do that?"

"Yeah, no standards."

"Total whore! Who does that?"

"Doesn't she think about the future?"

"Yeah, no guy is going to want a washed-up hooker."

And quietly I sit by. I am not a prude, but I'm not a slut either. Or am I?

To judge by what I'm hearing, I am. If they knew about me, what would they think, these friends of mine who have experienced so little but have so many opinions?

Mostly I just stay silent. It would be more trouble than it's worth to disabuse them of their illusions. These illusions, where do they come from? Is it envy? Ignorance? Or is it merely fear and aversion to what they don't know or understand? We fear the dark, because in its ebony folds, who knows what dangers lurk? I hold my tongue.

The strong prey on the weak; it's the lesson of natural selection. Rip them apart, drink from the pooling crimson of their exposed wounds. Nature is certainly a mother.

The jungle of the 21st century is not nearly so nice. The lions are still beautiful, but their bite is poison-tipped. Sometimes the lion or the lioness will take down its prey amidst the other beasts. It is a good way of asserting its power.

Of course, this is only how the poison begins to spread. It takes others to make it fester. Once the lionesses have made their kill and returned to their dens, the carrion-feeders descend. The real damage is only beginning.

Vultures and hyenas seldom make kills on their own. In fact, they are pack creatures. Together they swoop in and peel the remaining flesh from the victim's carcass. They will not attack alone, but together they can strip away what dignity is left.

It takes many forms, this feasting by the parasites.

Once the first shot is taken, more will follow. It takes the form of ending conversations when the person arrives, of moving to another seat in class, of challenging anything he or she says. It is passive bullying. No blows are struck or insults made. They don't need to be.

The weak see one weaker and it gives them a rush. *At last I am strong*, they think. *I am not the lowest of the low.* Then the awful truth hits them. *If he or she can fall, why not me? And what will stop them from rising again? I must not be the lowest of the low! If I can't be the best, then I certainly will not be the worst.*

It is self-preservation.

I suppose if I were to shed the guise of a bystander, I would be a middling-bully. I never seek to hurt someone, but I allow them to be hurt as long as it doesn't affect me. I am a potential victim. I have to watch out.

There are three players in this equation. The first is the bully. This individual holds a position of power. Then, naturally, there's the victim. They are the ones without control, the system acted upon by external forces. Finally, there is the third member of the ensemble, who is neither transmitter nor receptor. So where does the third person figure in?

Consider a juggler. The balls fly through the air, constantly mixing, constantly in motion. It is a balance. Up, down, and around. This is the circle; this is the metaphor. We are each of us in motion. The bystander cannot remain impassive. The victim will not always be on the receiving end of torment. The bully can be injured too.

Do we gain anything from bullying? We do lose so much. Especially those who perpetrate the deed. No one can hurt us so badly as we hurt ourselves.

Human relationships are confusing. It is so easy to hurt one another. Yet there will always be a balance. One cannot affect another without being affected themselves.

A Plea

Karina M. Dutra

A group had formed
Circled around a body.
The poor thing collapsed on the ground
Dazed, confused, ashamed.
The feelings it must feel.
I had only seen the aftermath,
This battle for survival,
The fight to stay alive,
The noises—Oh, those dreadful sounds,
The whispers, the laughter, the chatter.

Then the beast emerges from his pack,
He is fuming
Not with Anger
But with Pride.
He is just a pup
Yet dominates the crowd,
With the rest of them—his minions—
Only howling; cheering him on.

Then I see what I fear most of all—Tears
Tears begin streaming down the little one's face.
Panic strikes the crowd
But not the beast and his crew,

Their evil grins remain plastered to their dirty faces.

I scan the scene around me

Hurry—there isn't much time.

Pushing, shoving, screeching,

I make my way to the front.

See her lying there—Hopeless,

Bawling her eyes out.

I wrap my arms around her,

Tell her "Everything is okay, you're going to be okay."

Quickly the tears retreat back into the little one's eyes.

"Everything is okay."

As we leave the circle,

I take one glance back—

Eyes, the eyes of the beast are penetrating into my skull,

Threatening me without words,

Searching desperately for a look of fear in mine.

Knowing what I have to do, I give him one last look—

Disappointment?

Then I check her,

Cheeks flushed,

Stains of gray from where tears once lay.

I tell her one last time "Everything is okay."

She takes a wobbly heavy breath.

I do the same.

Blink, open my eyes,

And begin to walk among the wandering eyes,

Past the tire swing,

Past the lunch tables,

Past the monkey bars,

And wonder,

Why do we do this?

Why do they do this?

My seven-year-old mind cannot fathom the answers,

And I know the little one cannot either.

Can you?

Good-Bye, Happily Ever After

Maya Dehlin

I have always been more affected by stories than most. When I first heard of Noah's Ark as a child, I cried. It didn't seem right that God would let so many die, wicked or not. Years later, I flipped through the worn pages of *Grimm's Fairy Tales* searching for stories with that "happily ever after" ending. I became obsessed by the story of the poor goose girl, whose betraying best friend was punished graphically—her naked body placed inside a barrel with nails driven into it. She was dragged through the streets by a horse and carriage to warn the world of the consequences of wickedness. I was disgusted and never picked up that book again.

Classmates and friends always said, "Why do you care? It didn't happen to you!" Or, "It's just pretend. Get over it." But I couldn't.

When I got older, stories affected me on a different level. I couldn't brush off disturbing events anymore, claiming, "They're just pretend," because they weren't. When I learned about

Holocaust victims, persecuted simply because of their religion, I was horrified. The pain that humans could cause one another, willingly, was appalling. I suddenly likened the bullying I saw every day in school to that treatment of the Jewish people, with both fueled by bitter, ignorant hatred.

This was how I first befriended a social outcast. Steve got texts every day telling him that no one loved him and that he should kill himself. He believed them. What else was there to do, when he was so alone? One day, he asked me to proofread a letter. As I read it, I felt a searing pain in my heart. It was a good-bye letter to his parents.

"You have done nothing wrong," he wrote. "You don't deserve a son like me."

What could cause such self-hatred and despair? Why did Steve want to end his life? He was gay. The politics and religion of the subject aside, I knew there was absolutely no reason for any soul on this planet to feel such pain.

Through the years, I have heard too many stories—stories of abusive fathers, cutting, drugs, suicide, self-hatred, and loss of hope. At first, they were a burden. I would feel weighed down, which would lead to despair. Was there any good left in the world? Did people completely lack compassion? Was putting yourself in another's shoes unheard of? I would lock myself in the bathroom stalls and cry for this pain that wasn't even mine. But I guess in a way it was, because I felt so deeply for others.

Then, one day, Steve said to me, "I'm moving. And I want you to know that I'm grateful. Thank you for having the courage to be my friend when no one else would. Even though you are pretty and popular, you're the kindest person I know."

I have never received a compliment that came even close to that one.

People still tell me their stories. I hear tales of loss, anguish, and anger. The darkness still appears to be all-consuming sometimes, but now it doesn't weigh me down. Instead, I feel honored to hold people's stories and secrets. I am grateful for my gift— the gift to feel what others feel. Feeling leads to understanding, understanding leads to sympathizing, sympathizing leads to action, and with action, we can change the world.

Chapter Six

GUILTY CONFESSIONS

*"Knowing what's right doesn't mean
much unless you do what's right."*

—*Theodore Roosevelt*

My Problem with Piggy

Michael Fink

When it came to certain people at school, I walked around with my nose in the air. Call it self-righteousness for the sake of being popular, or whatever, but I had an arrogance that kept me from truly being the nice guy I always thought I was. Sure, I had plenty of "friends," but I wasn't always nice to them.

I especially picked on Piggy. He was a kid my friends and I let tag along so we could tease him. He was guaranteed entertainment. He got his nickname because we made snide remarks about his weight. Thinking back, the only reason I hung out with him was to make myself look better in a crowd.

Volleyball season came around, and Piggy showed up for practice. A friend and I were telling jokes and got laughing so hard that we started to cry. Then Piggy came over and slapped me on the back.

"You're the best, Mike," he said, choking with laughter.

Still carrying on the cheerful mood, I asked, "What do you mean, Piggy?"

He looked at me and grinned. "You're my best friend, man. You keep me entertained and everything!"

Those words could have killed me. I had never treated him with respect, yet he considered me his best friend. Needless to say, my happy attitude crumbled. Those words struck me like a bullet, and I vowed to treat him better.

I took small steps to change; for instance, I started calling him Gary instead of Piggy and encouraged him in volleyball. I got to know him better and realized that we had a lot in common.

Then, one night, this person I had once thought so little of became a much bigger part of my life. After a volleyball game, I offered Gary a ride home. As I was making a turn, a speeding car T-boned us on the driver's side. I panicked. Nothing but curses and frantic pleas for help left my mouth. It was Gary who ultimately took control of the situation. He put the car in park for me and suggested we get out to talk to the other driver.

She wasn't very pleasant; in spite of my panicked state, she yelled at me. I was still stunned, unable to believe this had happened. Again, Gary stepped in, calming the woman down and doing what needed to be done. I had put him through the wringer and probably made him feel horrible countless times, yet he was a great friend to me when I needed him.

Getting to know Gary has helped me to grow up. I've thrown all that superficial stuff out the window, and while others still tease him, I never make him the butt of jokes. Most important, I stick up for him because I owe him. Now, because of Gary's strength of character and loyalty, I know what it means to have a real friend.

No Speaking in Study Hall

Kaitlin Maloney

"Cockeyed ho," a voice whispers.

I am sitting in study hall, leaning over my work. I hear the whisper again and look up, then sigh with relief when I realize the words are not directed at me, but at someone behind me.

I hear the sound of a camera and realize that three girls are taking pictures of another girl. The teacher doesn't notice. I pretend not to either because I am friends with two of the bullies. I don't know the girl they're making fun of. I stay silent. Silence is easier.

But staying silent is not brave or courageous. I am a class officer, a student-athlete, a high honors student, a member of the student senate, someone who is supposed to be a leader, but I don't feel like one now. I am a coward.

As I listen to the torment behind me, memories flash through my head. I am back in my seventh-grade classroom, studying words with the prefix "bi-," listening to my classmates mock a boy for his bisexual orientation. He puts his head down and cries. I say nothing.

I go further back, to sixth grade. I see myself at the bus stop, yelling at a girl for dating someone I thought I loved. I give her a nasty look every time I pass her in the hallway.

Fifth-grade memories surface. My classmates are circled around me. People I thought were my friends are calling me names. Someone pushes me to the ground, and everyone starts kicking me. Tears threaten to spill over, but I will not let them. I have just "come out" to myself. I figure this is what I get for being gay.

The study hall phone rings, interrupting my memories. Apparently the victim left and went to the principal's office to report the girls. Now he is on the other end of the phone. I eavesdrop on the conversation. The study hall monitor is flustered. "They were all completely silent," she tells him defensively. Her oblivion angers me.

The three girls are separated, and study hall continues in silence. The bullied girl returns, and I contemplate passing her a note to apologize for not speaking up, but I never work up the courage. I am afraid one of the other bullies, my friends, will see me.

It has been three days since the incident. I have passed the girl a few times in the hallway. I haven't been able to bring myself to meet her eyes. I want desperately to say something.

I wish I could end this story by saying that I finally took a stand and supported this girl. I didn't. Most stories have a hero. This one doesn't. It only has a girl who still needs to learn how to speak out against bullying.

90 Minutes

Jonathan Dow

I *have better things to be doing*, I thought as I entered the gym, surrounded by friends filling the air with jokes and laughter. We were headed to a bullying seminar that would last two periods. I am not one to question an excuse to get out of class, but this assembly was during my study hall. I had a biology test to prepare for and a few overdue assignments, and I really didn't want to miss my free period.

But it wasn't just the unfinished school work that made me reluctant to attend this assembly; the topic made me uneasy. We were all a little on edge when our parents explained that some serious subjects would be addressed today, things that were rarely discussed openly with teenagers. A speaker, John Halligan, was going to tell us the story of his son, who committed suicide after being bullied.

Mr. Halligan began by introducing us to his son, Ryan, showing a slideshow with photos of a dark-haired boy as a toddler, a child, and then a teen. We watched as he slowly transformed from a happy kid into an awkward teenager. He had a strained smile—like a mask that hid his pain. Mr. Halligan told us about Ryan's early developmental problems, the bullying he faced, and his advice to his son.

Mr. Halligan's emotions changed as he told his story. His voice was full of affection when he spoke of Ryan as a child, then pain as he described Ryan's bullying and suicide, and then anger as he talked about the boy who bullied his son. He told us how Ryan had stood up to his bully, and the torment at school had stopped—for a while. He spoke of how Ryan had befriended the bully, sharing personal details with him. After that, the bullying reignited.

While he spoke, I stared at my running shoes, memorizing every scratch and scuff. Thoughts of homework were gone, replaced with a nagging sense of guilt. During these profound 90 minutes of my life, I thought about how often I had teased and humiliated others.

Mr. Halligan told us how his son's bully spread a horrible rumor about him. I remembered every rumor that had escaped my mouth. I thought of every sly comment, every joke that put someone in a negative light. Before you condemn me, consider honestly whether any of your actions might have been hurtful to another person. We have all been guilty of this at one time or another.

No one stood up for Ryan; bystanders abandoned him. I desperately wanted to believe that I would have defended him, that I wouldn't have been just another person in the faceless crowd who simply watched. But I already knew the truth: many, many times I had witnessed bullying and done nothing.

Mr. Halligan continued, telling us about a girl Ryan had been chatting with online, whom Ryan thought he had a special bond with. She later told him that she was just joking around and that she and her friends had laughed at his responses. Soon after, Ryan's sister found him dead, and his family's world was shattered.

Mr. Halligan ended by saying that since Ryan's death, he has been visiting schools to share his son's story. He spoke of the many supportive e-mails from students and parents he's received, and every time he heard that Ryan's story had changed someone, it helped heal the hole in his heart.

I can still remember that assembly as if I had just experienced it. The gym was filled with students but was totally silent, which eerily reminded me of the thousands of white tombstones and the stillness at Arlington National Cemetery. Some students were crying, some watched intently, some shifted uncomfortably in their seats, but everyone was affected.

Those 90 minutes changed me. I realized that what I once considered meaningless jokes could be a fatal poison for the target of my teasing. I was once an average teenager who used humor to get people to notice me, but now I know how much my words can hurt.

A Bully Alone

Monica A. Juarez

I am a bully. I was a bully.

Those are the hardest words I've ever said. I hurt others and didn't care. I actually laughed about the pain I caused.

Middle school was a breeze. I had friends who would pick on other kids with me. However, karma caught up with me when I got to high school. Suddenly I was thrown in with hundreds of others. Being conceited and cruel took a toll, and I learned the hard way that being a bully isn't the best way to make friends. In fact, it's the opposite. I became the isolated one. I needed to change. So I decided to apologize.

The first person I thought about was a girl I'll call Kate, whom I had bullied in middle school. A long, lonely summer later, I recalled all I had done to her with new remorse. I remember telling her she was nobody and to stop standing up for herself because no one cared. The next day Kate was punching holes in the girls' bathroom walls and crying because of what I had said.

Instead of feeling bad and stopping my tyranny, I laughed and used her emotional outburst against her. I took it even further and wrote things about her where I knew she'd see them. Ironically, I had friends then, people to laugh with, but when it was over and our victim had lost her will to fight back, I was the one left broken. Then who was the loner with no one to laugh with?

I had befriended the wrong people and believed they needed me as much as I depended on them. But my mean spirit backfired. Being a bully alone is like becoming your own victim. The

© 2013 Ellena Pfeffer

things I say to myself are worse than anything I ever said to Kate. Some people were willing to look past what I've said and done to them, but not Kate. And somehow I guess that's for the best. That way I can't hurt her again. I haven't yet forgiven myself for how I treated her.

From a distance, I can see Kate is happy. She has real friends now, ones who don't care if she cries or is made fun of. I envy her. Someday I hope to be that content with myself and the people around me.

Not Guilt Free

Kayla Colbert

I lead a relatively charmed existence in an upper-middle-class community in southern California. I'm not terribly outgoing, but I have enough friends to be content. And for the sake of full disclosure, I am biracial (of Caucasian and African descent) and openly gay. Nevertheless, I have never truly experienced any personal repercussions for unequivocally being myself.

My school is more or less an accepting place—a motley assemblage of students from every race, nationality, and creed this side of the Milky Way. I suppose you could call me a poster child for a postrace, postgay society.

I have never been bullied, honestly. But unfortunately I can't say that I've never taken part in bullying. When I was in middle school (the finest years for any individual, undoubtedly), I was catty and started rumors about other students. Ironically, I usually did this only to girls who were rumored or confirmed lesbians. I would involuntarily watch these girls every day at school, and I would feel this uncomfortable combination of envy and disgust in my chest.

To me, these girls represented things that I absolutely hated about myself. I was extremely self-conscious about my awkward adolescent appearance and the Narnia-deep closet I was in. To compensate for my insecurities, I spread venomous gossip until I felt better about myself. I wanted to punish these girls for daring to be themselves when I was too weak to. I was crippled by fear that the same sort of rumors would be used to attack me. I realized I was acting on my own insecurities, and I was even jealous of my targets.

When I eventually came out, it wasn't exactly ceremonious, but it was enlightening for me. I found that there will always be people who try to tear you down, but they aren't (and shouldn't be) the important ones in your life. And I didn't need to be that person anymore.

There's a boy I've seen around my school; he used to sit near my friends and me during lunch. His clothes are atrocious, he talks oddly, and he's always alone with a book. And while I know he might be considered "weird" by some, I can't help smiling every time I see him proudly rolling his backpack along the walkways. Being true to myself hasn't come easily, and knowing that someone else can do it too—no matter what others may think or say—gives me the courage to keep trying.

Four Chairs Down

Libby Sellers

"Why me?"

Teenagers ask themselves this question every day, wondering how life would be different if they were the head cheerleader, the star football player, or simply a person who is respected by their peers.

Sadly, this is not the case for many teenagers.

Tim always sat in the same place during lunch, four chairs down from my friends and me. He was always alone, always had the same little sandwich box, and always sat with his face angled toward the floor.

For weeks, I tried to get up the courage to talk to Tim and invite him to join our conversation, but I always found reasons not to. I made excuses like "My friends wouldn't be nice to him" or "He'd feel uncomfortable."

One day, a group of boys known for giving guys like Tim a hard time snuck up and stole his sandwich box. Tim got very upset and repeatedly asked them to give it back, but they just laughed.

I watched angrily, but I am ashamed to say I did nothing.

Finally, a girl walked over and yelled at the boys, snatched the box from their hands, and gave it back to Tim. He immediately gathered up his things and left the cafeteria. He never came back to sit at my table, four chairs down. I still regret not talking to him, and I wonder, if I had, would things have gone differently that day in the cafeteria?

Tim wasn't the only one who had a hard time at school. That year, just two days before graduation, a senior committed suicide. I vividly remember when we learned of his death. A hush fell over the school as we listened to our principal make the sad announcement over the loudspeaker. That boy must have felt so alone in the world, so unwanted, that he couldn't see a happy future, even after high school. I watched as everyone in my classroom grew still and silent. I wondered if anyone else was thinking about Tim and that day in the cafeteria.

Bullies are easy to blame, but they're not the whole problem. As the saying goes, "When you point a finger, there are three fingers pointing back at you." The people who don't speak up, like me, are also a big part of the problem. We don't stand up to bullies, because we fear having people think we're not "cool." We don't want to become a target ourselves. But a bully will stop if enough people stand up.

I know from my own experience that standing up to a bully isn't easy to do. But if we support each other against those who seek to single us out, we'll have a better chance of helping those who sit alone, four chairs down.

The Victim Speaks

Gemma Hahn

I won't mention her name, because to us, she never had one. We called her other names, instead—sharp, prickly thorns created with a swish of our tongues.

I wish I could say I didn't fit into the same category as those hurtful name callers, but I guess I contributed, since I was pretending the game wasn't happening. No, I was pretending that the game didn't exist at all.

I was new to the school, but right away I noticed the difference in my classmates' voices when they spoke to her. Only two or three classes had passed before I realized that to our peers everything she did was wrong. Soon, I found out why.

She couldn't speak English properly. She always got the answers wrong when she was called on by teachers. She didn't know when she wasn't wanted.

She deserved to be taunted, laughed at, and pushed around by the boys. She deserved having the girls spread rumors about her. She deserved everything her classmates did to her. Were they unreasonable? Were they cruel? No, of course not. It was just a silly game that gave everyone a laugh.

But it wasn't a game to her. Whenever I turned around, she would be looking at us, asking why. But I was a newcomer. What could I do? That excuse helped me ignore her sad stare. It wasn't enough, though, to wash away the guilt that stuck in my brain like gum.

Then one day she ended her silence and spoke her mind.

It all started during a group project in English class: a paper about manipulation and alienation. The teacher assigned me to work with my best friend—and her. I didn't want to work with her, but I had to do the project.

The three of us gathered in the front row to talk about the assignment. I was cautious at first. My friend laughed and smiled like she usually did, but the little crack in her giggle told me she was not so sure about this either. Our other group member remained quiet, as always, with that blank expression on her face. She giggled at a few jokes but mainly looked at her feet. Finally she said, "I want to do something on rumors and gossip."

Her words dug deep into my guilty brain. For some reason, I was scared. But I was a newcomer. I had no choice. I told myself I didn't have to like her to work with her. But the rest of our discussion was a success. We spoke like friends, laughed and giggled, jotted down notes.

Meanwhile, the game continued. One day all the girls ran to the English room and slammed the door in her face. Soon after, I went to the bathroom and could hear someone crying in a stall, so I hurried back to class.

I started to work harder on our paper after that. I did research. I gave examples. I added my opinion. Her sobs echoed in my ears as I worked.

I started to realize that I had a lot in common with the nameless girl. I was an outsider, like her, except she was braver. During our group meetings, she confessed her thoughts about how she had been treated, and I knew I could trust her. Our friendship strengthened. She volunteered to present our project to the class, and we agreed that she should.

Putting the finishing touches on our paper, I wrote the final sentence: "Even the simplest word slipping off a tongue can damage others terribly." After a moment's hesitation, I added: "Are you a murderer-to-be?"

The day of the presentation, I felt kind of sick. I imagined her up on stage, stuttering in a tiny voice, timidly looking down at her feet—maybe even bursting into tears.

Finally it was our turn. My heart slammed against my chest, and I felt like throwing up as she began to speak. Her voice was smooth, molten lava, every drop of anger now flowing. Her Korean accent was still there, but no one really noticed it. She talked directly to the audience, speaking the words we'd written together, emphasizing the blame and accusing the class for their malicious actions: gossip, manipulation, rumors, alienation. She often smiled—a cold smile that froze in the onlookers' veins. She was speaking for herself and everyone in her situation. She bravely pronounced words that most victims would be scared to say. If she was nervous or reluctant, she didn't show it. Her words flowed rapidly and naturally. Finally, only the last sentence remained to be said.

Even now, I remember that moment: how her eyes flashed, how she clearly pronounced each syllable—"Are you a murderer-to-be?" I was awed by her bravery and strength. How she had transformed from a weak little girl to a calm, angry adult. This presentation wasn't about revenge or rage, but a simple question for her tormentors.

She returned to her seat. The audience clapped reluctantly. I could see they were flustered by her final question. After class, they dumped their fears on her. They clustered around her and demanded, "What was that supposed to mean?" and "'Murderer-to-be' is a bit much."

I decided that it was time to make it clear that I wasn't in the same category as my classmates. I would no longer stand idly by as they tormented her. So I said, loud enough for everyone to hear: "I actually wrote that sentence."

Although it took all my courage to speak those words, nothing happened.

I was expecting questions like "Why did you do it?" or "What's wrong with you?" but my peers simply started talking about something else and walked away. She was alone again, but I knew she had heard me speak up for her.

At lunch that day I was sitting with my best friend as usual. Alerted by a strange feeling, I looked around. My eyes met hers, and we shared a small smile. We held that gaze for a moment, and then she returned to her solitude and I returned to my conversation. It was one of the greatest moments of my life.

The girls still whispered behind her back. The boys aimed for her when playing dodgeball. When the class threw a farewell party for me, she wasn't invited. Yet she showed me, showed all of us, a different side of her. She proved how strong she was. And that was good enough.

The relationship I shared with her was the strangest one I ever had, in a good way. I still don't want to mention her name. But she did have a name. It was a pretty name that suited her perfectly. And although I am not in touch with her, I have a feeling that she's perfectly fine.

The Spitball

Sharon Goldman

I can't forget that day in science class. I keep telling myself that I did the right thing, but sometimes I wonder.

We are encouraged to stand up to bullies, but speaking up is perhaps one of the hardest things to do. We fear being mocked or becoming a target ourselves.

There was a boy in my class who was picked on a lot. Let's call him Joshua. Joshua was kind, compassionate, and incredibly intelligent, but his learning challenges and social awkwardness made him an easy target for bullies.

One day, we were sitting in science class watching a documentary that nobody was paying attention to. Some students were doodling; others were passing notes. I was scribbling math problems behind my science binder, trying to get a head start on homework, with occasional glances at the projector.

A few tables down, Joshua sat with his eyes fixed on the screen. He may have had some academic challenges, but he had a genuine passion for learning. He was interested in all things science, which clearly made him an exception in this room full of distracted, apathetic teenagers.

Suddenly, a spitball flew his way. I saw him jump, turn around to see where it had come from, and turn back to the movie with eyebrows creased. I looked over to see two boys huddled together, pointing and snickering at Joshua. They were the kind of kids who thought learning was stupid. But their tall, muscular bodies and ability to get attention made them popular.

I felt a surge of bitterness but turned back to my homework, hoping they wouldn't do it again. But a minute later, another spitball flew over my desk toward Joshua's head. Once again, he spun around, trying to figure out who had done it.

At this point, the guilty teens were shaking with barely controlled laughter. I usually stay out of situations like this, but they were being so rude that I couldn't bite my tongue. I was about to say something, searching for the right words, when another boy spoke up. Pete was also high up on the totem pole of popularity, but he was kind and good-humored. He was universally liked and respected for his habit of complimenting others and making people laugh.

"Guys," he said. "That's not cool. Stop it."

The bullies looked at him blankly. I thought I could see the gears in their brains slowly whirring into comprehension.

"But . . . it's funny!" one of them replied with such justification in his voice that for a moment a cloud of anger blocked my vision.

"I don't care," Pete said calmly. "It's not cool."

At that moment, I butted in. My anger toward the boys was uncontainable. "Actually," I blurted, "it's kind of jerky."

I immediately cursed myself silently, and my cheeks flushed with embarrassment. *Jerky? Really? I had to say that?* I sounded like a little girl, and from the reaction of the two boys, knew I hadn't helped the cause.

They snorted into their notebooks, then threw up their arms simultaneously. "Oh!" they sneered, looking me over with mocking glares. I was a quiet girl whose shyness only faded around friends. I had never spoken to them before, and now I was awkwardly trying to say that they were jerks. How dare I—an unpopular nerd—comment on their actions? I felt my ears burning with embarrassment and looked back down at my notebook.

They continued to shoot spitballs at Joshua. My self-esteem was temporarily ruined, so I tried desperately to ignore their actions. Afterward, when everyone else had left, I approached Joshua, feeling guilty for not speaking up again.

"Don't worry about them," I said. "They're just disgusting." He nodded sadly. "Seriously," I told him, "you're much better than they are."

After that, Joshua changed around me. He asked me questions about school, looked over my notes, and treated me like a friend. He trusted me. This fact made me feel even worse. Didn't he see that I was incapable of standing up to his bullies?

We are told by some to stand up to bullies, but they don't really understand the repercussions of trying to do this. If I quietly and calmly state that what the bully is doing is "not nice," I will be mocked or ignored. If I stand up in rage and scream profanities at the bully, I will be labeled "overreactive" and "crazy." If I tell the teacher, I will be known as a tattletale (a term that does not, in fact, disappear after kindergarten). Even if I didn't care about my reputation, which I admittedly do, I wouldn't change anything by speaking up.

I have since been disrespected by those two obnoxious boys. I suppose I don't really care what they think, but I do care what Joshua thinks of me. I am kind and brave in his eyes, even though, in reality, I couldn't help him.

That is a day I will always regret. And yet, no matter how many times I replay the scenario in my head, I cannot imagine a perfect solution.

Strength for the Bullied

Kristen Noel Maxwell

They say you're lame, they say you aren't smart.
They say you are worthless, and end where you start.
They say you're not cool, they say you're a pity.
Don't let anyone ever say that you're not pretty.

They say you're ugly, they say you're overweight.
They say you're anorexic, they say you're not great.
They say you're emo, they say you have no worth.
They say to quit trying, they say your life is not deserved.

They say you take up oxygen, they say you take up space,
They say you're annoying, that you need to be replaced.
They say you're a retard, they say you're insane.
They say you're an infidel, they say you're to blame.

But you know deep inside you that you're not all these things.
That your life can be amazing, and you can achieve your
    dreams.
So, put down that razor. Put down that knife.
Step back, take a breath, and don't let them take your life.

Remember you're loved, remember there's care.
You have a shoulder to cry on anywhere.
Remember they're not worth it, the bullying will stop.
Wait for that day, and don't let yourself drop.

Your life may feel empty, your heart might break.
But it's not worth it, no matter the size of the mistake.
So, put down that rifle, put down those pills.
Don't stand in the road, don't let yourself get killed.

Write out your feelings, maybe punch a wall.
But life is worth it, so don't let yourself fall.
If this poem is all that pulled you through,
Know that I believe, and I reach out to you.

© 2013 Kayla Capps

My Guilty Addiction

Brittany Butler

Bullying is a hot topic right now—everything from minor incidents of harassment to physical violence and suicide. Most stories of bullying come from the perspective of the victim; rarely are they told from the viewpoint of the bully. I have never been perfect, nor will I ever be, and there are definitely blemishes in my past I wish I could erase. Bullying is one of them.

I am an inherently proud person, which affected my early friendships. I was unable to truly connect with others because I wanted desperately to stand out, to be better than everyone else. Even with friends, I constantly had to be superior. I would even find subtle ways to put them down and make them feel inferior.

Academics are the most important thing to me. I am ambitious. I love learning, studying, and discovering new things. And I am naturally good at these things. But there was a time when I took every opportunity to shoot down anyone who came close to me academically.

I knew what bullying was. Maybe what I did was not typical

bullying, but I knew it was wrong. Yet I couldn't stop myself. Once I started, the desire to stay on top was uncontrollable. My only thought was *I cannot fall. I must stay on top. I cannot lose my place.* My ambition had twisted into a gruesome obsession. I put others down to feed my ego.

Now that I can look back and reflect, I understand that my issue was one of power, domination, and ultimately control. Control is something I've always felt I lacked in life. Control over my surroundings, control in my family life, and control of myself. I had a monstrous inferiority complex because of my fear of failure. Dominating academically, even when it hurt others, was one way I felt control.

Bullying often spawns from fear or a feeling of inadequacy. And once a bully feels the powerful high of hurting others, stopping can be difficult. But the fact is, it was not just others I was bullying; it was myself. Once I realized my motivations, it was easier to change.

Bullying is a challenging problem. However, until we begin trying to understand the bullies, we will not address the issue effectively.

© 2013 Andy Fitzgerald

Hidden Pain

Luisa Aparisi-França

Fitting in at my school was difficult. Often, socially awkward kids would fill the friendless void with electronics. I remember one boy in particular, Ethan, who always brought his PlayStation Portable (PSP) to school. He was short and chubby, with spiky brown hair and big blue eyes. Ethan was considered awkward and boring. Sadly, the only time people interacted with him was when they wanted to play with his PSP. When he tried to talk to them, he was curtly told to "shut up."

I had algebra class with Ethan. While the teacher was writing on the board and most of us were taking notes, some of the boys would fool around in the back of the room. What they loved to do more than anything was harass Ethan.

I don't understand why everyone hated him. Sure, he would intentionally annoy people, but I think he did it because that was the only way he could get them to interact with him.

The boys would imitate Ethan and ask him questions that made him look stupid. It was like watching a cat play with a

176

mouse. Except in this case, the mouse never squirmed. As they took turns insulting Ethan, he would just smile and shrug his shoulders, saying he didn't care.

I secretly admired Ethan for handling it so well. It seemed he didn't need anyone to defend him; the insults just rolled off his back. It seemed like such a nonissue that even the teachers didn't bother to get involved.

But one day I learned that Ethan's inhuman resilience was a façade. In math class, I happened to look over and noticed that Ethan was methodically destroying his calculator. Snapping a shard of plastic, he pricked his thumb with it, digging it in deeper until blood welled up and began to drip onto his desk.

I was the only one who noticed. Horrified, I hissed, "Ethan, what are you doing?"

His answering smile sent chills down my back.

I told the teacher, and Ethan was sent to the nurse.

We all deal differently with our problems. Some people, like Ethan, bottle it up until they have to let it out in extreme or tragic ways. Many recent school shootings have been linked to bullying.

I wonder whether the little I did to help Ethan may have kept things from going that far. But I still think every day that I could have helped him sooner by reaching out. I wonder what would have happened if he'd reached his breaking point when he was alone.

My English teacher once told me that humans need three things to survive: their basic needs fulfilled, a belief in something bigger than themselves, and contact with other people. Ethan was desperate for that contact and had to do something to gain attention. I wish we had made it easier for him.

My Friends Were Bullies

Lily Seibert

I was lucky enough to grow up in New York City, a place where uniqueness is celebrated. My school had a mission to make children comfortable with expressing themselves. I heard stories of kids getting beaten up and having their lunch money stolen, but that seemed a world away. Things like that simply didn't happen here.

But that all changed in fifth grade. My class had a new student I'll call John, who had just moved from Korea and was new to America and its customs. I found him fascinating, and we became good friends. However, the rest of my class didn't accept him as readily. Kids took every chance to ridicule John about everything from the way he pronounced some of our words to his taste in food. I still remember hearing his anguished sobs from the bathroom. You don't forget something like that.

It was especially hard for me to watch John get bullied, since some of my best friends were taking part. For the first time, I was forced to choose between going with the crowd or doing what I knew was right. As much as I tried to stand up for my friend—and I tried very hard—the pressure from my peers was unyielding. Sometimes I found myself joining in without even meaning to. Anyone who says that it's easy to stand up to a friend is wrong. I know firsthand.

One Saturday afternoon a year after John arrived, he called to tell me he was leaving our school. As much as he assured me it wasn't because of how he'd been treated, I knew better. On our last day of sixth grade, we said good-bye, and I have seen him only once or twice since. I will always regret that I didn't try harder to defend him.

If someone you know is being picked on, it is so important to do what you can to stop it, because you never know when it will be too late. If you have trouble finding the courage to stand up to the bullies, comforting the victim can help him or her feel less alone. I wish I had done more to be a friend and comfort to John. I realize now it may have cost me our friendship. It could have cost John even more.

Now, in high school, kids are teased or belittled, but nothing comes close to what happened in fifth and sixth grade. I can't help cringing when I see a grade schooler being tormented on the bus. When that happens, John's agonized sobs ring in my ears, even after all this time.

Chapter Seven

BULLYING 2.0

"I would rather be a little nobody
than to be an evil somebody."

—*Abraham Lincoln*

When "Liking" Is Hateful

Erika Pell

In late February this year I became a victim of cyberbullying.

Someone created a Facebook page called "I Hate Erika." It had over a hundred friends who had "liked" hateful content posted about me.

Of course I read the page. The comments and wall posts claimed that I bragged about sex acts, which was entirely untrue, but my reputation was trashed as a result. The things people said about me were horrible, and it affected my real life, especially how I was treated in school. When I walked down the hallway I would hear death threats and people whispering behind my back. It was the worst time in my life. I kept my head down, trying to be invisible. My life was turned upside down.

I told my parents, who were horrified by what the other students had said about me. It killed them to see me going through such misery. When my mother printed out the Facebook account, it was thirteen pages of slanderous comments and hurtful remarks that made me feel as small as a pea. We took the evidence to the police and the school, requesting that the vice principal and my teachers stop this torture. But nothing seemed to work. No one was doing anything about it, and meanwhile it was killing me.

There were nights I would cry myself to sleep just wishing that my life would go back to normal. I became a darker person, filled with anger. I reached the point that I just wanted it all to be over, any way possible.

My parents finally said enough is enough. We set up a meeting with the principal and described the problem. His only suggestion was that I take a few days off from school to calm down and let things cool off. When it came time for me to return, I couldn't do it. I couldn't walk through those doors again knowing that even the principal wasn't really behind me.

So my parents enrolled me in a different high school, which wasn't an ideal solution. But since then, things have been great. I still have some tough times, but I don't face the same kind of bullying and I'm able to manage better. To this day, nothing has been done about my cyberbullying; we still don't even know who created the page, although I have a hunch. Even though no authorities helped fix the situation, I have moved on and am able to put the whole experience behind me and get on with my life.

My Facebook Bully

Audrey Miller

Allison. A simple name given to many people. But because of this girl, what began as a freshman year full of hope and excitement turned into one filled with torture.

All the years I've known Allison, she has often been mean to me for no apparent reason. I would go to school wondering which version of her I would find. So, one day, I got the cruel version of her, and I thought she'd be fine the next day, but one day turned into weeks, and she kept being awful toward me.

At first she just gave me dirty looks when we passed, which I tried to ignore. And I did ignore. But then one day I got a message from her on Facebook telling me she hated me and that I was a bitch. That bothered me; I'd never been attacked online before. I wrote back trying to defend myself and telling her I didn't understand why she was saying these things. I had done nothing to her. Well, needless to say, she didn't like that.

The messages kept filling up my Facebook. At first they were only from Allison, telling me what a slut she thought I was, but then I started getting messages from her friends. Then people who used to be my friends. They said I was a slut, a whore, a bitch, scuzzy, worthless, immature, pathetic, obnoxious, ugly, fat, and—the one that hurt the most—unlovable. I got ten to fifteen messages a day from Allison and her "crew," verbally attacking me online. This happened the first month of freshman year, so one month after school started, I was in the bathroom crying. That was eventually what I did every day during lunch. I cried in the bathroom. Alone.

Then I started los-ing friends. Eventually I had no one. And that was when I learned what it's like to be truly alone. I stopped caring about my grades or my appear-ance. School for others may have been fun, but for me it was hell.

© 2013 Maria Sweeney

I confided in a teacher about being cyberbullied. She told me to take it one day at a time. And she helped me realize I wasn't alone. Every morning I would go see her, just to talk. She always knew how to cheer me up, and I could see she truly cared. Sometimes I would go to her crying because of how much Allison had hurt me.

The summer before sophomore year, one of Allison's friends messaged me and asked if I would unblock Allison because she wanted to talk to me. So I took the chance and we became friends on Facebook again. And that's when the miracle happened. Allison apologized and asked if we could start over. I said yes. She meant what she said; to this day, she hasn't bullied me, and we talk daily.

To anyone struggling with cyberbullying, please remember that there is hope, and even though right now it might be hard to believe, things do get better.

A Call to Delete Cyberbullying

Caitlin Larsen

Death is something we all face eventually. It's something we have to deal with and accept because, ironically, it's part of life. We often associate it with old people who've lived long, full lives. But sometimes death steals someone too soon and needlessly, and it's difficult to accept. Amanda Cummings is just one sad example.

Fifteen-year-old Amanda lived in Staten Island, New York, and was tormented by peers who harassed her in school and on Facebook. Condescending and cruel words were flung at her—in real life and virtually—and convinced this beautiful girl with a bright future that she had no reason to live. She felt so worthless that two days after Christmas, she threw herself in front of a bus, a suicide note in her pocket. Her death forced her community to acknowledge the dire consequences of cyberbullying.

Bullying at school has always been an issue. Who hasn't had something bad said about them? Recently, however, bullying has expanded its grip to social networking sites. Unlike face-to-face bullying in school, there is no escape from cyberbullying after the last bell of the school day rings. Rather than home being a sanctuary, technology has turned it into an unchaperoned playground where bullies run rampant, completely hidden from teachers and concerned adults. Everything shared online becomes a target, and unlike face-to-face bullying, the torture can be seen and shared by anyone with access to the Internet. And worse, it can be revisited by the victim again and again.

Amanda Cummings is not alone. There have been too many stories in the media about teens committing suicide as a result of online bullying. In Amanda's case, even her posts where she was reaching out for help were ridiculed. She didn't want to report her tormentors because she was afraid the bullying would only get worse, so she decided to live with it. And then she decided she couldn't live with it anymore and had to stop it—the only way she knew how. Even when Amanda was in the hospital, before she succumbed to her injuries, bullies continued to post cruel comments on her Facebook page. If that wasn't heartless enough, the abuse continued on the memorial page set up after her funeral.

There is nothing we can do to help the teens who have ended their lives because of cyberbullying, but we can prevent more from succumbing to the pressure. We can help those teens who are beaten down. I challenge my fellow high school students to take a stand against cyberbullying. No matter how tempting or funny "jokes" at another's expense on social networking sites may be, don't take part in dealing out malicious comments or encouraging those who do. Stop and think about how you would feel if you logged on to find that others were making fun of you.

In my state of New York, lawmakers have taken steps toward classifying online bullying as a hate crime that will result in strong punishment for bullies. Reach out to your lawmakers and encourage them to create similar legislation. In the meantime, if you witness someone being abused online, take a screenshot and share it with an adult, whether it's a guidance counselor, your parent, or the victim's parent. Anything is better than staying silent; silence allows cyberbullying to continue and could result in suicide.

Let your voice be heard. Reach out to victims and tell them how much they are worth. Cancel out the millions of nasty comments with words of praise. Make victims aware of their value as human beings. Nothing is more important than a friend in dark times. You can be the one who helps someone find strength. Don't let anyone die believing they are useless. Let Amanda Cummings's story stand as a reminder of what cyberbullying can do.

© 2013 Peter Barell

Think Before You Post

Sharon Miller

In my third-period class, four girls sit across the room, giggling and making audible remarks about the social awkwardness of the girl next to me. They exchange eyebrow-raised glances when one boy asks a question they deem "stupid," and roll their eyes every time someone who's not part of their posse makes an intelligent comment. These meticulously primped girls are members of my school's untouchable elite, those social royals who decide what is right and wrong, whom no one really likes but wouldn't dare challenge either.

The self-appointed governors of my school's social scene control the senior parking lot, challenging any outsider who dares park in choice spots, forcing everyone else to the outskirts of the lot. They dominate the school's concourse, library, and classrooms, never letting their presence go unacknowledged. But worst of all is the way they abuse Facebook. They create exclusive groups and conversation threads and attack outsiders in forums designed to promote school spirit and class unity.

Late one weeknight, I logged on to Facebook only to find a cryptic post between two of these popular girls. Two others had "liked" it and commented on it, adding a sarcastic "lol" and tagging me in the post so it showed up in my notifications. Clearly, whatever they were laughing about involved me.

Cyberbullying is increasingly common. Posting critical comments about a person's behavior or appearance can make the victim feel inferior or guilty. "Cybershaming"—public chastising for behavior that's considered improper—is cruel and judgmental and is a dangerous form of cyberbullying. It comes wrapped in a package of "morality" so it's sometimes hard to pinpoint as bullying since so many people think the victim "deserves" it. And often the victim doesn't even know it's happening.

I promptly "de-friended" the four girls and the rest of their clique, hoping to rid myself of this memory and prevent similar incidents in the future. I couldn't decide what hurt more: that this joke was public or that I let it affect me so much.

In the months that followed, our school held several programs on bullying, including a powerful lecture on cyberbullying. Unfortunately, it went basically ignored by the student population, who continued online bullying. I have no doubt that if those girls were asked if what they did to me was bullying, they'd promptly dismiss the claim. To them, it was one wall post—a split second of typing with little thought involved. But to me it was a judgment, several tearful nights, a shameful few weeks in school, and an awful experience I will never forget. They had been confident enough in their social status that they felt no embarrassment in attacking me directly.

The Internet has many benefits, but unfortunately it can create a barrier between people, making interactions impersonal and allowing people to be mean without repercussions or guilt. All I can take from this experience is to be careful and thoughtful in my online interactions. My opinion of someone's behavior does not give me the right to shame that person. No words go unnoticed, especially online, where they're often frozen forever.

So please, think before you post. It will save me, and countless others, a great deal of heartbreak.

Anon Hate

Allyson Fontaine

"No one loves you, you know."

"Your family would be better off without you."

"Kill yourself."

These are all things I've seen said anonymously on the Internet.

As a member of the digital generation, I've reaped the benefits of modern technology, but I've also seen its shortcomings first-hand. The anonymity that social networking sites like Facebook and Tumblr provide can be truly terrifying; their "honesty box" and "ask box," respectively, enable users to say anything to one another without fear of being revealed.

In the time I've spent on these sites, I have not only witnessed cyberbullying between strangers, but I've comforted friends who have been victimized—and even received a few negative comments myself.

The truth is, today's society is rapidly changing. Tools unheard of thirty years ago are now a major part of our daily lives. Our society is still working out how to handle them, debating whether this technology is necessary and effective or a force that is ruining some aspects of humanity. At the very least, it has allowed people to act in a very different way.

This topic affects me. It matters to me. I've seen teen girls who struggle with depression, eating disorders, and abuse after being targeted and torn down by strangers who simply have nothing better to do or think it's funny. It infuriates me that anyone could think it's okay, because they're anonymous, to be so cruel that they actually tell a person to take their own life.

This issue has become increasingly critical among young people. Cyberbullying has already caused many deaths, including the well-publicized suicides of Ryan Halligan and Megan Meier. Sometimes I wonder if there is no sanctuary from such hatred; after all, Meier's tormentor was her neighbor.

However, for every online bully I've seen cause tears, five kind users have rushed in to dry them. Clearly, I'm not the only one who is angry over this outpouring of "anon hate," and I am grateful to the others who refuse to allow it. While the wounds caused by malicious words may remain, support and assurances of friendship can mean the difference between life and death for the victim.

Of course, it's not yet clear what impact technology will ultimately have on our society as it continues to advance. It may have already allowed some to act brutally, but I have faith that others will find ways to use it as a device for spreading kindness and good will. For example, I recently joined an online support network that provides help to those attacked online. After all, we are the digital generation. It's up to us to make the choice: be a part of the problem, ignore it, or join the effort to stop it.

I Want My Brother Back

Ellis Juhlin

He was pure
Innocence wrapped her arms around his shoulders
And purity whispered sweet nothings in his ear

You poisoned him

He was confident
With a laugh that was contagious
And a twinkle in his eye that always brightened
   my day

He was smart
The top of his class
Perfect As without a tinge of arrogance

He was my brother

That was before
Before you entered his life
Before you killed purity and took over for her
In his ear constantly
Convincing him he was never good enough
Convincing him no one cared
Not even me

You built a fortress around him
With walls of steel

Impenetrable to my tears
That even his family's love couldn't break down

You told him he was worthless
He fought you but you came back
With reinforcements

You egged our house
but
You rotted his soul

You reduced him to a shadow
Hesitant with everyone
Needing pills to get by
Coping became his way of life

He ran away
Too scared to return to school
His own chamber of torture
Where you and your cronies
Waited at his locker every day

He came back
But it wasn't the same

And even now that you're gone
That we finally pulled out every last root of the
    doubt you planted in him
There's an empty space that your lies once filled

A shadow of a boy
Who sits in silence
Most days

You stole my brother
And they can say you're a bully
But that name proves too light
To describe a monster such as yourself

I miss him every day
And it eats me up to see this face
So similar to how his once looked

It's not him

My brother didn't take antidepressants
Or see a therapist twice a week
My brother didn't wake up in the night screaming
Remembering what you did to him

Unspeakable cruelty

One day he'll come back
It's all I pray will happen
You took him
You broke him

We're helping him put the pieces back together
But it'll take years

I hope you look in the mirror and see the demon
    staring back

I just wish you could see things as I do
I wish you could watch guys strip your baby brother bare
And mock him until he became as pitiful as they'd
    tell him he was

I want you to have to run to his room
When he screams out in the night
I want you to sit outside his door and hear him sob
A boy who never cried before
I want you to turn the corner and see him sitting, staring
    into space with a look of horror
Tormented by things only he can see

Things only he can remember

I'll never know all that you
    did to him
But I know you do
I don't really want revenge
I want awareness and
I want my brother back

© 2013 Danielle Kardell

A Forum for Hate

Amanda Berg

Bullying seems to be an epidemic. One of the most recent advances in the world of its abuse is social networking sites, including Twitter and Facebook. Now, I admit I am an avid Twitter user. I love it and find it a great way to stay connected. But I was recently reminded of how destructive it can be.

At a meeting for my school newspaper, one girl suggested we do an article on bullying related to fashion. She mentioned a Twitter feed that was popular in our school but was causing problems. I had followed that page months earlier; it was originally created as a forum to share news about school events. To my horror, I learned that it was now overrun with kids posting nasty pictures and tweets mocking other students. I was appalled. Even kids I knew and respected had joined in. It had become a place to bully others.

I scrolled through months and months of the anonymous account, wondering how it could have gotten this bad. What's worse is that a lot of the victims were probably unaware that they were being publicly humiliated here.

As I continued looking through the feed, I found some acts of heroism. Some brave students had tried to make the problem-page's followers aware that they were being bullies and their actions were plain wrong. Sadly, they had just made matters worse. Students began to tell the heroes that it was their right under the First Amendment to say whatever they wanted, and that their free speech couldn't be shut down.

Not everyone realizes that your constitutional right to free speech does not apply to harassing others in school, at school events, and on school-sponsored forums. In addition, national debate rages over whether to create limits on free speech on the Internet. Legal aspects aside, cyberbullying is morally wrong and can cause depression, anxiety, and even suicide. There are too many cases where young people have committed suicide as a result of online harassment. Bullying does not have to be face-to-face to be painful, damaging, and long lasting.

So from one teen to another, knock it off. We all get mad sometimes. But we must remember to think before we tweet, post, or text. When in doubt, remember the Golden Rule. Nobody wants another person's death hanging over their head because of online drama. It just isn't worth it.

In Defense of the Golden Rule

Sarah Shi

For years, I've seen posters hanging on the walls at school, reminding us of the Golden Rule—"Treat others the way you want to be treated." Obviously, the message hasn't sunk in.

Currently, with social networking sites like Twitter, Facebook, and Tumblr, it's too easy to let "friends" in, and the sad result is that a new form of bullying—cyberbullying—has taken the main stage in the teen world.

There are many ways these sites can be exploited by bullies. For instance, they can anonymously create Facebook pages dedicated to mocking peers and posting unflattering photos for others to comment on. This happened at my school. A small circle of students created a Twitter page titled "Here to talk about shit." And what they did there was exactly what the name implied. They wrote disturbing comments about peers, personal things that weren't meant for the Twitter world. The bullied students told our school counselors, even printing out the page as proof, but because the founders of the page remained anonymous, the counselors could do nothing.

Believe me, teens won't pay any attention to posters urging them to be kinder toward peers. And although high schools are implementing bullying-awareness programs, students don't take them to heart.

Cyberbullying is permanent; once you hit "enter," the words can't be erased or taken back. I believe the best way to address the problem is to find ways to let peers step into one anothers' shoes and take the time to understand how their words and actions, even the most minute ones, affect others. Simple words can go a long way. Make them go the right way.

Chapter Eight

INSIDE ME

*"A man who does not think
for himself does not think at all."*

— Oscar Wilde

The Hell I Endured

Katherine Dolgenos

I'm not even close to being overweight, yet I cannot bring myself to wear a bikini. I monitor my weight religiously and avoid fattening foods. If the scale goes up at all, I sink into depression. If I lose even a pound, I am ecstatic. I am this way because I was bullied.

It is difficult for those who haven't been bullied to understand how completely bullies can dominate the lives of their victims. A bully's most effective weapon is his or her ability to make victims feel utterly worthless. It can be a slow process; for me, it took a few years to be worn down.

First, the boys in my class began to taunt me. They called me fat, ugly, and retarded. I pretended to ignore them. "Boys don't matter to me," I announced confidently. That was a lie. Of course their opinions mattered to me. When my crush told me he didn't find fat girls cute, I felt like curling up in a hole and dying.

The girls were subtler than the boys. They never insulted me to my face. They just stopped talking to me, one by one—first the popular girls, then the others, and finally my best friends.

When the teacher would tell them to include me, the girls reluctantly complied, rolling their eyes and making me feel as unwelcome as possible.

My rejection by the girls emboldened the boys. In sixth grade, one boy kicked my ankles whenever I participated in class. He was expelled after he pushed me into a pond. My classmates held a good-bye party for him during lunch, which I was not invited to; one boy explained that my attendance would be awkward. I sat alone on the playground, wishing I could go home.

Was my lowest point when my mother suggested I invite a friend to the movies and I couldn't think of a single person who would accept? Or was it when I tried to make myself throw up, but couldn't and cried because I wasn't even a competent bulimic? Maybe it was when my exasperated teacher told me to stop bothering her at recess and go play with the other kids.

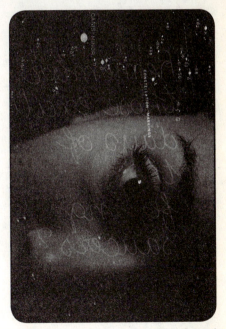

I was convinced that if I just lost weight, everything would be better. Now I know that it wouldn't have made a difference, but I learned that the hard way. Because of the bullying, my mind-set is permanently

© 2013 Chloe Sheppard

changed. I can't eat without calculating the calories. I can't pass a group of snickering girls without pulling down my shirt, sure that they're laughing at my hips. I literally walk blocks out of my way to avoid passing the houses of girls from my old school.

I am cringing at the thought of anyone I know reading this. I am writing it only because it is important that people know this: bullying affects victims for years afterward. I will remember these events for the rest of my life.

When All You Hear Is Black Noise

Daria Etezadi

I cannot say anything, not really. I want to, but what would I say? Adults tell us that kids are cruel, so we just learn to accept the cruelty and roll with the punches. We get used to people mocking others openly, physically intimidating them, posting degrading pictures on the Internet, and so on. But that's not how I'm bullied.

I have not been physically assaulted or verbally attacked, my locker has not been bashed in or plastered with demeaning stickers, and no one ever stole my lunch money.

Yet I have experienced silence.

Bullying is an art form. Traditional types of bullying, like physical intimidation and overt name-calling, are almost easier to accept because there are clear responses for victims: fight back if you have the strength, or walk away if you have the power.

But victims of "silent" bullying can't fight back or walk away. It's much harder to call out bullies who use exclusion to target victims. This type of bullying is a specter you can't point to or fight against.

I remember a time when my classmates read a list of people invited to an upcoming party and deliberately skipped my name. And when they cast disapproving looks in my direction because I wore the same jacket every day. And when I ate my lunch leaning against a wall day after day because none of the cliques would acknowledge me when I asked to sit with them.

Silent bullies need to know that when they ignore a peer's existence, they are saying that that person is not worth their time or attention. And silence can be even more damaging than taunts and punches.

Silence possesses an unspoken power, and yet silent bullies are rarely held accountable for their cruelty. They don't think they deserve any blame because they never said or did anything. Their victims can't point to anything specific that they did. But there is an unmistakable presence, the undeniable existence of something—a black noise that seeps into the victim's world and drowns out hope.

Amid all of this black noise, it takes only one voice to say something—one voice to break the silence. But nobody says anything.

Past Imperfect

Cameron P.

Let me confess: I was a bully. It is a part of my past that has shaped me and, regrettably, probably shaped my victim. I wish I could go back and change what I did to the boy I harassed, but that is not an option. Instead, I do my best to embrace my guilty past to ensure that I am a better person now.

Bullies look for excuses to justify their actions. I was no different. My friends found what I did entertaining. They never spoke out against me, which encouraged and enabled my cruel behavior. I often told myself and my friends, "He's so annoying, he deserves it," or gave similar reasons why my victim was "asking for it." I put another person down based on his inherent, unchangeable characteristics and then forced him to shoulder the blame for my cruelty. I can remember only one time that a friend confronted me about something I had said. As usual, I blamed the victim. If he weren't so annoying, maybe I would leave him alone. It was a coward's excuse.

Bullying allowed me to feel powerful. Coming from a larger-than-average family, I always felt overshadowed by my siblings, who had achieved the same things I had—only years earlier. I was never the first or the best at anything. But in the cafeteria, surrounded by my peers—my equals—I found a way to get attention, raise myself above others, and feel good about myself.

Now that I'm older, I look back and see a different version of myself. A version that thought it made me "cool" to put down someone in front of friends. A version that thought it was acceptable to belittle one of my peers. A version that is in stark contrast to who I am now.

I can see the damage my comments made, and I'm ashamed. I now look for the positive in others and try to be as good a person as I can to everyone I interact with, no matter how small the encounter. While I can't change the impact I had on that boy in my past, I know that changing my attitude has made me a positive force for those around me now.

© 2013 Alicia Murphy

What I Know

Addison Nozell

I know that look
That sneer
That sense she has that she is something and I am not

I know that push in the hall
That "accidental" trip
Showing all that she is so strong, she can move others
    in her path

I know that tiny bit of paper
Words written to another
Telling someone else that I'm a loser because I can't
    kick the ball like her

I know that type of girl
I also know that she's wrong

Because she doesn't know me

She doesn't know that I volunteer to help others
I capture indoor bugs and release them to live their lives outside
And that I cheer for the team even though I'm not and never
    will be the best player

Every time she chooses me as the brunt of her attacks
I try not to, but I wither a little more

A vine without water

But what she especially doesn't know is that ultimately I am the
 strong one
I have a family and friends who care about me
Who tell me that mean people should not define who I am
I am the only person who can do that

They are my cool drink of water, restoring my roots to face
 another day

And I know they're right.

Our Own Worst Bully

Shefain Islam

One sneer, one "harmless" joke, one snide comment is where it all begins. A single act of bullying multiplies, spreading like a virus with no apparent cure, giving birth to hundreds of self-loathing thoughts in the minds of victims. The virus seeks an opportunity to get inside the vulnerable and self-conscious. In other words, it has infected almost every teenager and created an epidemic among youth today.

The virus is bullying. It has evaded the efforts of adults to stop it. As a teenager and current sufferer, I want to share a secret that many teenagers are too embarrassed to reveal and that may offer some insight into this disease. The secret is that bullying also comes from within.

Everyone is his or her own worst bully.

Adults who say high school is the best time of our lives obviously don't remember too well. High school is quite possibly the worst time for a young person's self-esteem. Every bulge, breakout, and blunder is observed and attacked. Kids can be vicious, and it takes only one act of bullying to spread the virus, launching a string of self-loathing thoughts. One chuckle from a popular girl can make a teenager self-conscious to the point of insanity. We begin to obsess about our perceived faults and repeatedly punish ourselves by overanalyzing every detail, from our hair to the way we walk. Maybe, we think, if we find our faults first, it won't hurt as much if someone laughs at us or insults us. We become our

own worst bullies, even if no one is actually mocking us.

All it takes is one look or taunt, and paranoia takes over. Our own minds whisper that we are constantly being laughed at and judged. That we're not good enough.

Understanding this paranoia and grief is important. We may not be able to stop others from being mean. Teenagers are quick

© 2013 J. H. Yue

with an unkind word, no matter how many bullying seminars they are made to sit through. However, insecurity and self-loathing are within our control. In order to beat bullying, we must stop the bully inside our heads.

We must encourage teenagers not to hate themselves and launch a campaign of self-love along with initiatives to fight bullying. The combination of love and a no-tolerance policy for bullying can destroy this virus for good.

Abuse Did This

Annika Ariel

I stare at my fingernails, ragged and bloody from my nervous bit-ing. My lip is numb from being chewed. My legs are shaking, which I hadn't even noticed until now. My eyes dart around, though I'm not sure what I'm looking for.

"Stand up straight. Get your hand out of your mouth."

I can't stand up straight, oh God, I can't. Don't make me. Please don't make me. My mouth opens, and I try and form words, but I fail. A nagging voice inside my head says, *You weren't always like this.*

And the truth is, I wasn't. I wasn't always nervous, fearful, and shy. Bullying contorted me into a beaten-down person, afraid to confront either my abusers or adults who are supposed to help me.

The abuse started when I was seven. Children my age told me I was better off dead. Once, the principal gave me a lollipop. But as I enjoyed the treat, one of my tormentors slapped the stick, jamming it into my mouth. The sweet taste was quickly replaced with sour blood.

When I was thirteen, a boy tripped me in the hall, and the fall

215

shattered my elbow, for which I needed surgery. I tried to tell a few adults what had happened. I was shocked when no school administrator was willing to help me, even when several students expressed concern. Since then, I've developed a stutter, especially when talking to adults.

The week after my elbow surgery was the band field trip to Six Flags. I had really been looking forward to it. When we got there, I set off the metal detectors since I had pins in my arm. I stammered my explanation to the guard, but had to be frisked. People stared. I started crying. My arm ached, and I wished I had stayed home. It didn't get any better once I was in the park. Because of my cast I couldn't go on any rides. I felt like I was being punished because a boy decided to trip me for a laugh. I spent most of the trip weeping while my bully spent the day having fun.

When I got home, I told my mom I had a great time.

I don't get bullied every day anymore, and I've made friends. Most of them don't know about what happened to me, and I want to keep it that way. Children may have been my tormentors, but adults stood idly by, aware of what was happening. I still am uncomfortable around adults, but I'm trying to learn to talk to and trust them again. I practice conversations with teachers in front of mirrors. I've even gotten speech therapy.

This year, I went to an amusement park with the band again. When I rode on the biggest roller coaster, I conquered my fear and excitedly told my band teacher what I had done. Without stuttering. Without fear. With trust, for once. And I will never forget what he said.

"I'm proud of you."

(Not) Born This Way

Sam Connan

Most people think bullies victimize others because they are just born mean, horrible people. That's bull. Kids bully because they're in pain; they need love they aren't getting. I know. I was a bully once.

I have attention deficit/hyperactivity disorder (ADHD), which makes it hard for me to stay still or think before I act. I have more control now, but before I was diagnosed, people just thought I was a bad kid. As a result, I had no friends, and everyone at school was afraid of me. I was a physical bully, but there was another kid who bullied with words, and I was his favorite target.

There was so much pain, sadness, and anger inside me, and I needed a way to let it out. I started hurting kids for no real reason. At first it was over little things, but it got so bad that I actually whipped one kid with my belt, hit another over the head with a shovel, and tried to strangle another one.

After years of wondering why I acted the way I did, my parents and I learned that I had ADHD. I started therapy and medication,

© 2013 Kyra L. Carmack

and things got much better for me. A big turning point for me was when the kindest, most popular kid in my class decided to sit down and talk to me. I asked him why and he simply said, "Everyone thinks I'm so cool, and they want to hang out with me, but you're the one I really want to hang out with." I still tear up when I think about that moment; to this day, I don't think he knows just how good it made me feel that he reached out.

I have friends now. In fact, the kid I strangled is now my best, most loyal friend. It's not that the doctor found some miracle drug that fixed me; I still have to work hard in therapy, and I still struggle, but the medicine gives me those crucial milliseconds to think before I act.

My point is that there is no such thing as being born bad. There's usually something else going on. Find out what it is, help that kid, and you will have changed one "bully" for the better.

Dear Peers

Sitav Nabi

Dear Peers,

I used to look up to you. I used to try to get your attention. I used to want to fit in by wearing what you wore and listening to all the lies you'd tell me. I used to laugh at jokes that weren't funny. I used to let you copy off my tests. I used to want to be like you.

Dear Peers,

I used to get very upset when you started rumors about me. I used to cry about it. I used to try to defend myself. I used to raise my voice, and when you didn't listen, it would ruin my day.

Dear Peers,

I used to get angry when you swore at me, when you cornered me and made up lies. I used to get mad when I walked into class and saw your scowls. I used to curse you back.

Dear Peers,

I used to hate the way you looked at me, as though I was less than you. I hated how you put down my ethnicity. It wasn't funny. I used to insult you under my breath for being so narrow-minded. I used to tell the teachers and you'd call me a snitch.

Dear Peers,

I used to ignore you. I used selective hearing, which you called a "big word." I stopped listening to your senseless language, without meaning, without dignity. I watched you stoop lower and lower for your own self-satisfaction. And then I opened my eyes.

Dear Peers,

I used to feel sorry for you. I pitied you when you made fun of my A while you got an F. I felt bad for you because you couldn't see the meaning in what mattered most. No, you were interested only in dating, clothes, cliques, and texting. It used to break my heart.

But not anymore.

Dear Peers,

Say what you want. Do what you want. Go ahead! Make up a rumor about my secret Internet boyfriend. Tell everyone I'm a "retard" who thinks the whole world is made up of textbooks and teachers. Throw paper balls at my head while I'm reading. Shoot me with pieces of buttered bagel at lunch. And then tell me what you got out of that. Do you feel superior? Was it fun? Do you think you've knocked me down? Has my smile gotten any duller? Does my family love me any less? Have my teachers stopped appreciating me in class? Did I lose any inspiration?

I used to be afraid of you. But not anymore.

Breaking Free

Katie Allowatt

I sit here

Alone

Unwanted

Betrayed

My tongue longing to speak words

But nothing changes

I'm silenced

What?

Did you hear that?

Everyone is talking

I can't breathe

I'm choking

I'm dying here

And you just watch

I sit here

Confused

Still

Quiet

Afraid to say anything

Because we all know

You wouldn't understand

You point
You laugh
You talk
But you don't think
You're killing me

Stop it
It hurts
My tears race down my face
In hopes of finding a happier place
Shh
You hear that?
That's me
Breaking free

Get to the Root

Emma Platoff

I have heard it said that this world houses two types of evil people: those who commit evil themselves, and those who see evil being done but do nothing to stop it—bullies, direct and indirect. In my life, I have been both.

Long-standing competition with my siblings left me perpetually argumentative and always ready to snap. The most trivial comment would set me off. I couldn't handle criticism, even when it was meant to be helpful. I spent so much of my life feeling less than my siblings, being excluded from their parties and talent shows. So when I got to middle school and was somehow—finally—accepted and liked, I used my influence in the wrong way.

I remember when a girl called me fat (after I had made a few choice comments of my own). She was driven, humiliated, from our lunch table after I turned her insult around, telling her there was obviously no room for her, given my apparent obesity. For weeks, I watched my friends ostracize her just as I had, taunting her with the methods I had taught them and enjoying my "win" wholeheartedly.

The victims of bullying have a better story to tell than the bullies—one that is more heart wrenching and easier to sympathize with. It's easy to see that bullying results in overwhelming problems. Figuring out ways in which authority figures can limit bullying and help victims is certainly the relevant—and perhaps the most important—action to take. But since it's a two-person interaction, how can we ignore the instigator?

I propose that instead of just focusing on victims, we seek to stop bullying at its root: the bullies themselves.

It's commonly believed that bullies hurt others because of their own insecurities, and I agree wholeheartedly. However, by explaining this to the victim, we're hoping to raise the victim up by bringing the bully down. Isn't that hypocritical? Isn't it, in fact, counterproductive to teach a victim the ways of the bully?

Undoubtedly it can be comforting to understand the origin of an unprovoked attack, but how does teaching a victim to belittle a bully not encourage him to become one himself? Knowing about a bully's weakness may empower victims, but I suggest that we also find ways to boost insecure people before they become bullies.

Afterword

Dr. Ramani Durvasula

Who cares?

If high school is "just high school" and kids are just being kids, then why try to enact change?

We have often assumed that teasing is part of coming of age, that it's a rite of passage, or a normalized hazing ritual. Where do we draw the line? When does it qualify as bullying? There is no easy answer to that, and, as a result, schools, parents, educators, and governments have had diffuse, disorganized, and often anemic responses to this crisis.

We can start by listening to teens' voices.

Young people have been teased for every trait or habit imaginable—appearance, clothing, race, sexual orientation, religion, disability, money, accent, interests, hobbies, and many times for reasons that made sense only to their victimizers. Whether this bullying has "always been with us" or not doesn't make it right.

These teens' stories are poetic and heartbreaking, uplifting and anguishing. These are not professors tossing out statistics. These are not movie stars doing a public service. They are just regular kids enduring and perpetrating a range of taunts and traumas then translating them into powerful writings.

What I read often left me wanting. What else happened? Did anyone get in trouble? Who exactly was to blame? How could you forgive? The air of mystery makes sense; sometimes we don't get to know how things turn out. How many of us know what happened to that kid in high school who was brutally taunted all those years ago?

I think the "holes" in these stories lend tremendous insight into why we often do not offer these victimized and victimizing children enough help in a timely manner. Even if we are paying attention, we see only part of the picture.

Bullying represents a painful and unique puzzle. Typically, the guidance that parents and educators give children is sound advice; it keeps them safe and helps them achieve goals. However, far too often, the sensible advice from adults when it comes to bullying—such as "communicate with your bully," "speak to the school," "let me talk with the parents"—doesn't work and it often leads to even more disastrous consequences. This leaves parents feeling powerless and terrified in the face of their child's victimization. So we wring our hands and wonder, *how can this happen?* When it does, we should also wonder, *What else can our kids do, and what else can we do for these kids?*

The young people featured in this book offer their own advice to their peers, both simple—just ask, *"How are you?"*—and courageous, such as confronting a bully head-on. Their suggestions, and the depth and realism of these suggestions, translate into adults' lives as well. These kids don't offer the sugar-coated reality that we all hope for and that the media too often promulgates. One brave confrontation is rarely enough to change it all: it takes hard work, day after day, fighting back against the disapproval and cruelty to break out on the other end.

Sometimes adults have been responsive and have worked to be the strongest allies of children and teens who are facing bullying. At other times, they have been ineffectual. Far too often, it appears that tragedy, trauma, and threat all could have been either averted or at least minimized if everyone had their eyes open, listened, and drew together.

The crystalline voices of these young people are a call to arms. So how can we help?

This can be won, but it means that none of us can phone it in anymore. We have to open our eyes and not just look, but see; not just listen, but hear. There *are* things we can all do.

Changes in patterns mean something is up. If a teen or child's sleeping habits, eating habits, academic performance, or even interaction patterns change, that's your cue to stop and talk. Change is a wakeup call—heed it.

Watch their health—headaches, stomachaches, bad dreams, or relying on illness to avoid school. If there is a shift from the usual, talk with them. Before you go to the pediatrician, call ahead and indicate that you want the doctor to ask for some alone time with your teen. Your MD may be able to get to the bottom of things faster than you.

Look at your kids—are their belongings coming home damaged? Are they coming home with unexplained scratches or wounds? Do they say they no longer want to go to school or walk to school? Talk to them, and also approach the school, but do so delicately and in a way that respects your child as well. He or she is likely afraid that this will lead to retribution.

Talk to your children about technology and online spaces. Many kids may find themselves joining the crowd out of curiosity and the desire to belong. Teach them that an online interaction is no different from an in-person inter-action, and that kindness and respect are not an option, but a necessity. Electronic echoes are forever, so discuss with your kids the damage to their futures and the lives of others that can ensue from careless communication.

Find a privacy balance. Kids using computers are minors with very powerful tools in front of them. Our kids know more about technology than we do and can find ways of going "underground" if they sense they are being over-monitored.

Be the change you want to see. Watch yourself and ensure that you aren't being a bully, acting in an entitled manner, or evidencing disrespect. Dignity and respect are behaviors that are modeled. They do as we do, not as we say.

Be aware of your schools' policies, and weigh in. Make sure your children's schools have good Internet safety procedures in place.

Know your child's peers. They are often rich sources of information and guide your teen's behavior. Respect them, learn about them, and listen to them. Isolate your child's peers and your child may slip away from you.

Keep in mind that even if you observe some of these patterns, it does not mean your child is necessarily being bullied. It may also indicate other issues that bear attention such as depression, substance use, or other interpersonal struggles. However, all of these still require us to step up and talk with our children so we can keep them safe and healthy.

The Young Authors Foundation

Established in 1989, *Teen Ink* is a monthly print magazine, book series, and website written entirely by teens for teens. All the royalties from the sale of this book are donated to the foundation.

Teen Ink magazine has been embraced by teachers, librarians, parents, and teenagers nationwide. Our eight books in the Teen Ink series are all written by teens and give great insight into the life and times of today's young adults. TeenInk.com is the largest website of its kind on the Internet.

Teen Ink empowers teenagers by publishing their words and works. It is also dedicated to improving reading, writing and critical thinking skills while encouraging creativity and building self-esteem. After reading more than 850,000 submissions from students over twenty-four years, the editors have published more than 65,000 works in the print magazine alone and hundreds of thousands more online. There is no charge to submit or be published, and all students published in the magazine or in books receive a free copy plus other gifts.

In keeping with its mission, the foundation also distributes class sets and individual copies to schools nationwide. In addition, some schools support the foundation by paying a small amount for their monthly class sets.

From its beginnings as a small foundation with a regional publication, The Young Authors Foundation and *Teen Ink* has grown steadily and today is a national program funded with subscriptions, individual donations, sponsorships, private grants, and advertising. In addition to the print magazine and books, Teen Ink runs the following programs:

TeenInk.com includes teen fiction, nonfiction, poetry, art, photos, book, movie and music reviews, college essays and reviews, contests, videos, resources, teen forums, and much more. The website includes all the past monthly issues of the print magazine and anyone can go online and request a free sample issue. Teens and adults also can follow Teen Ink on Facebook and Twitter.

Teen Ink's NYC Writing Program is a two-week intensive creative writing program for teenage girls ages fifteen to eighteen from around the country and overseas. The students are housed in The Juilliard School dorms and have daily classes, workshops, guest speakers, and enjoy the city sights and Broadway shows as background and inspiration for their writing.

Teen Ink Online Writing Courses are available to teens on a regular basis throughout the year. Courses focus on creative writing and creative nonfiction. Details are on TeenInk.com.

Teen Ink Poetry App for the iPhone allows students and adults to choose and read a teen-written poem that matches their daily moods.

Teen Ink Educator of the Year Contest welcomes nominating essays from students to honor outstanding teachers with cash prizes and publication of the winning essays in the magazine.

Teen Ink Interview Contest encourages teens to interview family and friends, with some students chosen to interview national celebrities—among them, Hillary Clinton, Laura Bush, Colin Powell, Steve Martin, Whoopi Goldberg, Alicia Keys, John Glenn, Jesse Jackson, Maya Angelou, George Lucas, and others.

The Teen Ink Books capture the essence of what it means to be a teenager today. *Teen Ink: Our Voices, Our Visions* was the first book in the series, and other books include *Friends and Family*, *Love and Relationships*, *What Matters*, *Chicken Soup for the Teenage Soul* (with all stories from Teen Ink authors), and *Written in the Dirt*, a book of fiction and poetry written by teens.

The Young Authors Foundation Inc. is the nonprofit 501(c)(3) organization that publishes *Teen Ink* and runs all the above programs. You can learn more about us on our website, TeenInk.com.

Teen Ink has publishing opportunities for teens. Any student age thirteen to nineteen is welcome to visit our website and to submit their work for publishing consideration. Each year we receive, read, and respond to more than 125,000 submissions from teens who want to be published in print or on our website.

Want to participate in any of the above programs? See the next page for details on how you can become a member of Teen Ink, support our foundation and programs, submit work for publishing consideration, and/or receive a free monthly copy of the magazine.

Contact Teen Ink and The Young Authors Foundation:
Address: Teen Ink, Box 30, Newton, MA 02461
Email: Editor@Teenink.com
Phone: 617-964-6800
Website: TeenInk.com

Join The Young Authors Foundation and get a monthly subscription to the
Teen Ink print magazine.

How to Submit to Teen Ink

Submit Your Work Through TeenInk.com

Submitting your work to Teen Ink has never been easier. Simply go to
TeenInk.com and hit the "Submit Work" button. All work submitted will be
read by our staff and considered for publication online, in our monthly print
magazine, and in future Teen Ink books. There is no charge to submit or to be
published, and all those published receive a free copy of the magazine or book.

Submitting Art or Photos

It is now very easy to submit your digital images and videos to TeenInk.
com. Just go to TeenInk.com and hit the "Submit Work" button. All art and
photos will be viewed by our staff and considered for publication online, in
our monthly print magazine, and in future Teen Ink books. Please send art
and photos at the highest resolution possible. All videos are also reviewed by
our staff before going live on the website.

Submitting a Video

Want to be part of our video campaign dedicated to teens telling their
personal stories about bullying? Visit TeenInk.com and click on "Video" then
"Bullying."

Plagiarism

Teen Ink has a no-tolerance policy for plagiarism. We check the originality of all published work through iThenticate, and any submission found to be plagiarized will be deleted from our site.

Anonymity

If, due to the personal nature of a piece, you don't want your name published, we will respect that request, but we must still have all name and address information for our records.

Gifts

Teens published in the print magazine will receive a complimentary copy of the issue containing their work. Teens published in our books also receive a free copy. All published authors/artists get an official congratulatory letter and other gifts.

Submitted Work Becomes the Property of Teen Ink

By submitting your work to us, you are giving Teen Ink and its partners, affiliates, and licensees the nonexclusive right to publish your work in any format, including print, electronic, and online media. However, all individual contributors to Teen Ink retain the right to submit their work for nonexclusive publication elsewhere, and you have our permission to do so. Teen Ink may edit or abridge your work at its sole discretion. To prevent others from stealing your work, Teen Ink is copyrighted by The Young Authors Foundation, Inc.

Bullying Resources

Disclaimer: *Due to the dynamic nature of the Internet, any web addresses contained in this book may have changed since publication and may no longer be valid.*

WEB RESOURCES/ORGANIZATIONS

Befrienders Worldwide
http://www.befrienders.org/
A registered charity with a site that features the world's most comprehensive directory of emotional support helplines.

The Ben Cohen StandUp Foundation
http://www.standupfoundation.com/
An organization that funds grants for other nonprofits' antibullying work.

Be a STAR Alliance
http://www.beastaralliance.org/
This group produces free resource kits for teachers and also provides students with information they need to start an antibullying group in their schools.

Born This Way Foundation
http://www.bornthiswayfoundation.org/
This foundation, created by musician Lady Gaga, has an interactive website featuring multiple ways for those who have been bullied to artistically share their stories.

BullyBust: Promoting a Community of Upstanders
http://www.schoolclimate.org/bullybust/

A "nationwide bully prevention awareness effort" that sponsors contests and hosts relevant web content for students, educators, and parents.

BullyPolice.org
http://www.bullypolice.org/
A watchdog organization with a large, comprehensive online list of U.S. states and their antibullying legislation.

Cyberbullying Resource Center
http://cyberbullying.us/
This nonprofit, directed by two professors of criminal justice, runs a site that contains advice for those who want to stop cyberbullying. It also freely distributes the professors' original research on the topic.

Facing History and Ourselves
http://facing.org/
A huge compilation of educator resources that focus on social justice and relate bullying to events that have occurred throughout history.

GLSEN: Gay, Lesbian and Straight Education Network
http://www.glsen.org/
The national organization that has created efforts like No Name-Calling Week and the Safe Space Kit, GLSEN also conducts publicly accessible research on school climates for LGBT youth.

It Gets Better Project
http://www.itgetsbetter.org/
An initiative that archives hundreds of videos created by LGBT youth and their allies, all supporting the message that "it gets better."

Mean Stinks
https://meanstinks.com/
A website compiling a series of answers to antibullying "challenges" (ranging from posters to suggestions for videos to ideas for positive chalk graffiti).

National Bullying Prevention Center

http://www.pacer.org/bullying/

The sponsor of National Bullying Prevention Month, this group also publishes multiple videos, stories, and other resources about bullying online for free.

Not In Our School

http://www.niot.org/nios/

A more-than-decade-old nonprofit that helps students create antibullying events and groups in their schools.

Reach Out

http://us.reachout.com/

A compilation of support information, with lots of articles written for and by teens.

Stand for the Silent

http://www.standforthesilent.org/

This group travels around America, offering school presentations then encouraging students to start their own chapters of the Stand for the Silent program.

StopBullying.gov

http://www.stopbullying.gov/

This educational website produced by the U.S. Department of Health and Human Services contains thorough definitions of bullying and cyberbullying, as well as techniques to use to stop them.

Stop Cyberbullying

http://www.stopcyberbullying.org/

Take a quiz to find out if you are part of the cyberbullying problem. Then read this site's guide to netiquette (online etiquette).

Stomp Out Bullying

http://www.stompoutbullying.org/

A campaign with a website containing a chat helpline and supportive messages from celebrity and teen "ambassadors."

That's Not Cool

http://www.thatsnotcool.com/

This public education campaign gives tips for what to do when someone you're dating, or someone you've dated, is harassing you via the Internet.

A Thin Line

http://www.athinline.org/

Comprehensive website with advice on how to combat cyberbullying and digital harassment, aimed at people who might be perpetrators as well as those who are being attacked.

"To This Day"

http://tothisdayproject.com/

A spoken-word piece by Canadian poet Shane Koyczan that has been adapted into a virally popular animated video.

To Write Love on Her Arms

http://www.twloha.com/

A mental health–focused nonprofit that sponsors multiple initiatives: campaigns that students can run in their high schools, a conference, benefits, and blogs.

TransYouth Family Allies

http://www.imatyfa.org/

This organization's website contains many useful resources for young transgender, transsexual, and gender-variant people and their parents.

The Trevor Project

http://www.thetrevorproject.org/

A national organization that runs a free hotline and chat service for LGBT youth who are in crisis or suicidal.

MOVIES

Adina's Deck

http://adinasdeck.com/

A multi-episode series for young teens about cyberbullying (as well as plagiarism and Internet predators).

Bully: The Movie

http://www.thebullyproject.com/

An indie documentary that follows the lives of five bullied kids in U.S. schools that has a website and book.

Bullied: A Student, a School, and a Case That Made History

http://www.tolerance.org/bullied

A 40-minute documentary about homophobia that the Teaching Tolerance project provides to educators for free.

Cyberbully

http://abcfamily.go.com/movies/cyberbully/

This original film by ABC Family has a companion website promoting their Delete Digital Drama campaign.

That's What I Am

http://www.imdb.com/title/tt1606180/

A 2011 coming-of-age movie following a bully and bystander in school in 1965.

BOOKS

Bazelon, Emily. *Sticks and Stones: Defeating the Culture of Bullying and Rediscovering the Power of Character and Empathy*. New York: Random House, 2013.

Beck, Debra. *My Feet Aren't Ugly: A Girl's Guide to Loving Herself from the Inside Out*. New York: Beaufort Books, 2011.

Bornstein, Kate. *Hello Cruel World: 101 Alternatives to Suicide for Teens, Freaks and Other Outlaws*. New York: Seven Stories Press, 2007.

Belleza, Rhoda, ed. *Cornered: Fourteen Stories of Bullying and Defiance*. Philadelphia, PA: Running Press Teens, 2012.

Hall, Megan Kelly and Carrie Jones, eds. *Dear Bully: Seventy Authors Tell Their Stories*. New York: HarperTeen, 2011.

Gardner, Olivia, Emily Buder, and Sarah Buder. *Letters to a Bullied Girl: Messages of Healing and Hope.* New York: Harper, 2008.

Hirsch, Lee, Cynthia Lowen, and Dina Santorelli. *Bully: An Action Plan for Teachers, Parents, and Communities to Combat the Bullying Crisis.* New York: Weinstein Books, 2012.

Miller, Terry and Dan Savage, eds. *It Gets Better: Coming Out, Overcoming Bullying, and Creating a Life Worth Living.* New York: Dutton, 2011.

Jacobs, Tim. *Teen Cyberbullying Investigated: Where Do Your Rights End and Consequences Begin?* Minneapolis, MN: Free Spirit Publishing, 2010.

Kaufman, Gershen, Lev Raphael, and Pamela Espeland. *Stick Up for Yourself: Every Kid's Guide to Personal Power and Positive Self-Esteem.* Minneapolis, MN: Free Spirit Publising, 1999.

Simmons, Rachel. *Odd Girl Speaks Out: Girls Write About Bullies, Cliques, Popularity, and Jealousy.* San Diego, CA: Harcourt, 2004.

Vanderberg, Hope, ed. *Sticks and Stones: Teens Write About Bullying.* New York: Youth Communication, 2009.

——, ed. *Vicious: True Stories by Teens About Bullying.* Minneapolis, MN: Free Spirit Publishing, 2012.

About the Editors

Stephanie H. Meyer, senior editor of *Teen Ink* magazine for twenty-five years, holds masters' degrees in education and social work and has dedicated her life to the welfare of youth. As the creator and senior editor of the widely recognized Teen Ink book series including, *Teen Ink: Our Voices, Our Visions,* she has culled through thousands of bullying essays and was amazed by their honesty and pain. She and her husband, John, have two children. To learn more, visit www.TeenInk.com.

John Meyer, MBA, is publisher of *Teen Ink* magazine. He works to keep the business side of the magazine functioning and has spearheaded the evolution of Teen Ink's website.

Emily Sperber has been an editor at *Teen Ink* for five years and has worked in publishing for fourteen years. Emily feels a particular connection to this book because as a young person, she often experienced and witnessed bullying. She hopes teens will find encouragement and hope within these pages, and that it will help them endure, stand up, or make a change for the better. More than anything, she wants readers to realize that their lives will change in ways they can't yet imagine after high school, and it's worth sticking around to see. Emily lives in Massachusetts, with her husband and two young children.

Heather Alexander is an editor of young adult books at a major publishing house in New York City. She finds the topic of bullying prevalent in every genre she works in, from contemporary to fantasy and sci-fi, and she knows it's something everyone can learn from. In literature, villains are overcome through love and understanding, and Heather thinks the same is true of bullies. She hopes one day to find bullying only in historical fiction. Heather lives in New York.

Contributors

Katie Allowatt is a songwriter and music fan from the Pacific Northwest. She enjoys the freedom of the outdoors, and her favorite place is the ocean. Katie wrote her poem, "Breaking Free," as a response to bullying experienced during middle school; she'd like to spread awareness about how other people may be feeling. She would like to thank her family and the English teacher who inspired her to submit to *Teen Ink*.

Damiana B. Andonova is living in pursuit of a childhood dream—to become an obstetrician—and believes that nothing should stop other kids from realizing their dreams. She writes children's books, likes to paint, and also works as a research assistant and babysitter. Damiana is saving up to take her sister to Tahiti! She dedicates "Standing Up for Simone" to Simone, Ellie-Jane, and Evelle, and to children everywhere.

Luisa Aparisi-França wrote the piece "Hidden Pain" about a classmate who was being tormented. She loves traveling, painting, and singing in the shower.

Annika Ariel is a clarinetist who plays in her town's youth orchestra, her school band, and many honor bands. She wrote "Abuse Did This" and wants to offer a sincere thank-you to her mother and to the music teachers who have influenced her. In addition to being a dedicated musician, Annika competes with her school academic decathlon team and teaches a creative writing class for middle-school students.

Peter Barell shot his photograph on a trip to Denmark, where he was introduced to members of an autistic community there. He is currently studying film on Long Island. He thanks Camilla, Simone and Mette for letting him take their picture.

Jack Bentele contributed "Sympathy for the Devil" in the hope that his perspective would be unique and helpful to other students. He has since overcome the trauma of middle school and is now studying screenwriting. In his spare time, he likes to run, but also to eat afterward and watch too much TV. He thanks his parents, Ray Bentele and Kathleen Gibbons.

Amanda Berg is an aspiring journalist who writes for her school newspaper. When she's not writing, she's busy with a service project or volunteer activity, and she also plays flute and piccolo as well as studying piano. Amanda found *Teen Ink*'s call for submissions just after discovering an abusive Twitter page and saw the chance to write "A Forum for Hate" as a perfect opportunity to combat cyberbullying. She'd like to thank all her English teachers, who, over time, have made her the writer she is today.

Kaitlyn Blais is currently an engineering student and enjoys running in her spare time. When she was 11, she was adopted into a family of seven sisters and one brother. Although she wrote "We Can't All Be 'In'" as a response to a class assignment, she says that the experience of creating the piece helped her come to terms with a memorable part of her childhood. Kaitlyn dedicates her piece to all bullies.

Julie Block is a field hockey player, participates in multiple extracurricular clubs, and has starred in ten school productions. She'd love to travel the world, and especially looks forward to someday seeing Broadway shows. Julie wrote "And It Keeps Swinging" to make people feel less lonely during times of sadness, especially when it is related to bullying. She thanks her junior year English teacher, Mrs. McHugh, for telling her about this opportunity, and her parents for always believing in her.

Autumn Bornholdt is a powerlifter and dancer, and also holds a black belt in karate. Her family is currently host to a French foreign exchange student. Autumn wrote "Slip 'n Slide" from the need to share a difficult experience with other teens. She thanks Mrs. Nelson for pushing her in class!

Maggie Brooks loves to explore—whether in mountains, her own street, or the world—and always travels with a book. She hopes that her words in "Enter Girl" will bring her experiences to others and wants to make them aware that bullying can be stopped, rather than simply ignored. Maggie thanks her family for all the adventures they let her take.

Rebecca Brown loves design, typography, unicorns, and photography. Her picture was taken at an old townhouse. She thanks Mitchell Davis for inspiring her to start taking photos.

Elana Burack hopes that her story, "My Frenemy," will empower victims to take control of their lives and allow bullies to see the effects they have on others. She dedicates her time to teaching—tutoring kids in Hebrew for their bar and bat mitzvahs, and helping adults with basic math and English skills. Elana believes the world would be a better place if more people smiled. She would like to thank her mom, dad, and sister for being the most loving, supportive, and brave family that anyone could have.

Brittany Butler loves academics and literature and also enjoys playing video games and working with computers. She has a black belt in karate. While writing "My Guilty Addiction," Brittany wanted to stress that bullying isn't a one-way street and that understanding the mind and reasoning of the bully is just as important as attempting to prevent bullying from happening: there are many different circumstances behind those who bully others. Brittany thanks her mother, and Ms. T., her English teacher.

Kayla Capps is majoring in technical photography at Appalachian State University. Her photo was inspired by the love of the pictured couple, Maddie and Aaron, for each other. She would like to thank them for booking photoshoots with her over the years, and also thanks her mom, dad, and boyfriend, Derrick.

Kyra L. Carmack based her art on a short story called "The Protectors" that she wrote for her eleventh-grade English class. She says, "Thank you, Mrs. Coburn, for everything that you taught me and for introducing me to the Teen Ink website."

Rachel Chevat based her poem, "The Worst Thing About Bullying," on her experiences of being bullied during middle school. She would like to thank the true friends who stuck by her during that time. As well as writing poetry,

Rachel is passionate about music; she has played a few shows of her own song-writing and has recently started selling her music as well.

Lamisa Chowdhury graduated high school in 2012. She wrote "Thanks, Jacob" to awaken compassion in her peers. For Lamisa, nothing beats a hot cup of tea and a candle burning in the background—her friends call her an addict! She hopes to work in the healthcare field one day. Lamisa would like to dedicate this piece to "Nathan," for opening her eyes, and to her parents for their limitless and loving support.

David Chrzanowski is currently attending college. During high school, he most enjoyed working with his high-school marching band, a welcoming program full of talented and diverse kids. He thanks his girlfriend, Moira, and his American lit teacher, Ms. Helwig, for helping him fine-tune "The Orange Bracelet."

Kayla Colbert is a columnist for her school newspaper, works as an intern at her local Chamber of Commerce, and volunteers for a food bank. She loves to read poetry near an open window on a sunny summer day, although her piece for this book, "Not Guilt-Free," is prose. Kayla wants to thank her teachers, Mr. Billings and Ms. Le, and also sends along a shout-out to the *MC Sun* newspaper staff.

Sam Connan would love to act on Broadway someday but is also interested in deep sea exploration. When he first started to write "(Not) Born This Way," it was just a school project, but he says that as he worked on the piece he realized for the first time just how good of a friend his best friend, Logan, has been. He dedicates it to Logan, to his parents, and to Rayna Dineen and Rosemary England.

Claire Davis is a dedicated Harry Potter fan and ferocious soccer player who also loves chocolate, *Doctor Who*, and spending time with her friends. She hopes that more teens will realize the good in standing up for others as well as themselves. Claire dedicates her poem, "If My Pillow Could Speak," to her mom.

Summer Davis originally wrote her poem, "The Smallest Star," as part of a play about bullying. Summer plays many instruments—piano, clarinet, percussion, mallets, and the bassoon—and is a member of multiple bands. She also loves horseback riding and hiking, and participates in her school's drama club and forensics team. She thanks her friends and family.

Maya Dehlin is a fifteen-year-old vegetarian. She loves playing tennis and the guitar, baking, and especially traveling, and hopes to eventually become a graphic designer in New York City. Maya wrote "Good-Bye, Happily Ever After" to promote love and acceptance for everyone in the world—not just the people most like us. She thanks everyone who's inspired her along the way.

Janna Dimopoulos spends her free time making YouTube videos. Her photograph is a self-portrait. Janna says of the image, "People stereotype me because of my body modifications. In actuality I'm just a shy nerd, and this photograph is an example not to judge a book by its cover." She thanks her family.

Elizabeth Ditty is currently a 19-year-old college sophomore majoring in early childhood education with a concentration in English and a minor in psychology. She plans on going to graduate school for counselor education. For Elizabeth, writing is an outlet: a safe and healthy way to vent without being afraid of judgment and to reflect on memories that can be uncomfortable to discuss. She dedicates her pieces, "Never Again" and "Kids, Meet the Real World," to her mother, sister, late father, stepfather, and Momma Taylor.

Katherine Dolgenos has lived in the same city her entire life, but hopes to study international relations and live abroad someday. She's already learned some Korean from online soap operas and has spent six weeks in Seoul, living with a host family and taking Korean classes. Katherine thanks her parents, Chelsea, and Isabella. She says that writing "The Hell I Endured" was "very painful, but it was worth it to me because I thought it might help someone else."

Jonathan Dow wrote "90 Minutes" in ninth grade after receiving the assignment to write about a major moment in his life. He swims on his school's boys' varsity team and rows at a boat club in Rhode Island.

Karina M. Dutra wrote "A Plea" because she believes it's important to address the bullying kids face even before middle and high school. She is an artist, working with photography as well as painting and drawing, and has been particularly inspired by a trip to France she took in 2011.

Ashley E. graduated from college in 2010, but wrote "The Christmas Tree" at the age of 14. As an adult looking back on it, Ashley says she is still amazed that other people could make her feel so awful. But she also believes that her struggles have brought her to a place of being stronger, smarter, and more compassionate than ever. Ashley would like to thank her family for always being in her corner.

Kenzie Estep loves using writing as an outlet and enjoys playing guitar and singing as other means of self-expression. She also participates in Key Club and mock trial with her school, and in her spare time she likes to hang out with friends and family. She wrote her piece, "The Bullet," as a response to a difficult time in her best friend's life; they want this story to help other people who are dealing with this and to hopefully stop it from happening to someone else. The work is dedicated to Kenzie's best friend, and she also thanks her family, friends, and eighth-grade English teacher.

Daria Etezadi has worked as the editor of her high school's newspaper and literary magazine, and she also has a passion for piano, which she's been playing for the past twelve years. Daria's piece, "When All You Hear Is Black Noise," is influenced by her experience of moving; she says, "As a new student in a new school in a new city, I felt as though I had lost my identity." In the future, she plans to advocate for the rights of Middle Eastern women to obtain an education. Daria thanks her mom.

Kaylee Euler was inspired to contribute "If We Were Allies" to this anthology because of her former experience as a victim of bullying. She participates in 4-H and Quiz Bowl and is a Harry Potter fan. Kaylee also loves to write and is involved in a writing club.

Emily C. Farrugia contributed "My Friends, My Bullies" as a way to let out intense emotions. After reading other people's experiences of bullying, she also wanted to take part in helping people become more aware of what bullies can be.

Kathryn Ferentchak graduated high school and is off to college. To keep herself relaxed and focused, she practices yoga daily. Her other hobbies include painting and photography, and she is especially interested in cinematography. Kathryn dedicates "A Walk on the Wild Side" to those who know her best, but even more to those who don't. "For a race of unique individuals, we are an awful lot alike," she says.

Michael Fink wrote "My Problem with Piggy" eight years ago, and much has happened since: he graduated from college with a degree in graphic design—he now works as an in-house graphic designer for a Fortune 500 company! He is happy to report that his friendship with "Gary" has continued through the years, though they are on opposite ends of the country and don't get to see each other often. He dedicates his piece to Anthony Garrison.

Andy Fitzgerald is a psychology student at the University of Illinois with a concentration in biopsychology. His photo was inspired by loneliness and the sadness that comes with it, and is also related to bullying, as he was bullied for eleven years.

Allyson Fontaine is now a college student, having graduated from high school in 2012. She is an aspiring equestrian who volunteers weekly as a veterinary assistant at a local humane association. Allyson thanks Armistead Lemon for her feedback on her piece, "Anon Hate."

Meia Geddes graduated high school in 2010 and currently attends a university, where she's begun a pen pal program with a friend. She wrote "Dear Friend" in high school, as a journal entry, while thinking back on more difficult days. Meia thanks Anna and all of the other beautiful people who have touched her life, and she hopes that those who read her work are inspired to be like her friend.

Sharon Goldman wrote "The Spitball" three years ago, while struggling with the question of how to be a positive ally to classmates who are bullied, and she is now glad to say that it does get better. Sharon is passionate about world affairs (she's lived in six countries), politics, reading, and backpacking, and she also volunteers at a local library reading with kindergarten students. She wants to thank her eighth-grade language arts teacher, Mr. O, who gave her confidence in writing.

Maya Gouw contributed two pieces of art to this book. She takes great pride in being an artist, as it's one of the few things to keep her going, and she dedicates her pieces to any victim of bullying.

Gemma Hahn wrote "How Are You?" in the belief that it would help people who were bullied, or are still being bullied, to know what she learned. She has a variety of hobbies: acting, singing, drawing, and, of course, reading and writing. Gemma has lived in a number of countries, including South Korea, Morocco, Russia, and the United Arab Emirates. She wants to thank her family for being with her through everything.

Megan Haddox says of her piece, "Devin and I weren't close or anything, but his loss really hit me hard. Everyone needs to hear his story. Rest in paradise and enjoy the cookies, Devin!" She thanks the Bradley family for letting her share Devin's story. Megan enjoys photography and writing and loves to watch baseball and spend time with her friends and family. She recently graduated from high school.

Sarah Hamel has been an activist since she began high school, attending rallies and protests and even participating in a sit-in. Her favorite form of activism is teaching, though, and she believes that being at a rally is nothing compared to spreading knowledge. Sarah's mother taught her the term "rhino skin," giving her a name for her shield, and Sarah wrote this piece to point out that inner strength is just as important as outside support. She thinks that having faith in things getting better is not enough; people need to believe they are strong.

Caitlyn Hannon is a college student who loves to camp during the summer with her family, bake crazy desserts, and hike in the woods. She's a fan of cheesy '80s movies and a piercing enthusiast. Caitlyn wrote "Pushed Too Far" because bullying can happen to anyone, anywhere, anytime. By sharing her story, she wanted to show other teens that even if they feel powerless, they are stronger than they think. She dedicates her work in loving memory to her cousins, Kelly and Danny.

Gwen Harrison is an actress who also loves to play soccer, read and write, and participate in volunteer work. She hopes "Living Hell" can help someone else overcome bullying. Gwen would like others not to see her experience as tragic, but to view it as as inspiration to stand up for those who need it.

Sandy Honig is a staff photographer for *Rookie* magazine and is enrolled at New York University. She thanks Margalit Cutler.

Lily Houghton would like to spread awareness about the bullying people with disabilities face. She dedicates "The R-Word" to her loving family, especially her brother, Henry, the strongest person she knows. Lily graduated high school recently and will be attending college soon. She loves theater, shopping, writing, Ireland, swimming, and any type of tea.

Robert Hwang has loved video games ever since he was a child, and as a senior in high school, he united with a friend to found a video game club. "King Worm" wants people to know that, although bullying comes in many forms, there is still always a light at the end of the tunnel, no matter who you are. He says, "Thank you, Mrs. Brown! I would not have made it this far without your support. You rock!"

Shefain Islam grew up in a big family, is on the quiz team at school, and likes to cook, bake, and read. She has recently become interested in classic Bengali literature. Shefain loves to travel and has been fortunate to visit a few places, but her "to do" list for spots to travel is endless. With "Our Own Worst Bully," she tried to offer a solution to the troubling thoughts and feelings that arise from bullying. Shefain would like to thank her family for all their support, especially her sister, who encouraged her to submit her piece.

Jenica Jessen is a reader, writer, Mormon, science-fiction fan, traveler, baker, thespian, former Samoan resident, mountain lover, and didgeridoo player. When she was first assigned a different lunch period from her friends, she sat alone in the cafeteria for a few days and suddenly noticed how many other kids sat alone too. Jenica's poem, "The Solitary," was inspired by this experience. She dedicates it to Camille, Erin, Adam, Matthew, and Rachel.

Monica A. Juarez wrote "A Bully Alone" as an apology to her peers and to any other kids being bullied. She thanks Jacqueline and her entire family. Monica loves reading—she considers it a sport, like a one-person race—and at school is involved with the Gay-Straight Alliance and Environmental Club. She also collects Bob Dylan memorabilia and enjoys adventures with her friends and older sister.

Ellis Juhlin adores animals and spends almost all her time volunteering at a local animal shelter. She comes from a very artistic family, but unable to draw to save her life, she has turned to painting pictures with words. Ellis writes often and is the editor-in-chief of her school's literary magazine, *Catharsis*. In "I Want My Brother Back," she wanted to share her perspective on bullying as one indirectly affected by it. She thanks her mom, dad, and brother.

Danielle Kardell wants to show others through her art that they are not alone in their pain and suffering, that someone out there cares for them deeply, and that they can persevere through trial. She thanks her mom, Michele.

Anton Largaespada created his drawing with a white colored pencil on black paper; it's a self-portrait he made for his tenth-grade drawing class. He chose to draw something that portrayed a universal emotion many teens feel. He dedicates his piece to his loving, supportive, and creative family.

Caitlin Larsen wrote "A Call to Delete Cyberbullying" shortly after a young girl in her community committed suicide, in part due to cyberbullying. She believes that because young people are the ones who started this, they are the only ones who can stop it. Caitlin once wanted to become a taxi driver in order to converse with lots of different types of people! She says, "As I grew older, I transformed my dream into a more realistic goal—writing. Writing gives me the ability to reach out to others, and just like in my taxicab, I find that people can be transformed, happier, and inspired by my words."

Jaemin (Joseph) Lee remembers feeling alone as a freshman and wants people to know there are many who are ostracized, each with their own stories. In "Befriending My Bully," he wanted to let people know that things do get better: that bullies and the bullied grow and are able to make a difference in the world. Jaemin's family is from South Korea where being gay is considered a mental illness, but he says that his relatives have had the open-mindedness to accept him. He grew up speaking English and Korean, is now proficient in five languages, and likes to cross-dress and wear animal onesies in his free time. He thanks his mother, sister, stepdad, John 2, Mr. Hankison, and Kevin.

Megan LaColla Linquist would someday like to freight-hop around the country with her journal and camera. She participates in debate and forensics as extracurriculars, and she loves music, words, and Turkey the country. Megan wrote her poem, "Nobody's Power," for everyone who is considered a "nobody," so that they won't let the wrong words make them feel invisible. She thanks her parents and best friend, Alex.

Kaitlin Maloney is a spoken-word poet who is also involved in the youth commission, class board, activities planning board, and various other extra-curriculars at her school. She writes for her school's newspaper and works as a camp counselor during the summer. Kaitlin's dream is to eventually serve as a United States ambassador. She decided to share her story, "No Speaking in Study Hall," after realizing that the bystander's perspective is often not taken into account. She would like to thank the family, teachers, and friends who have encouraged her to share her experiences through poetry and prose.

Jessica Martin graduated from college in 2008 and has recently moved back to the Philadelphia area, where she loves her job at an education-focused non-profit. When she's not working, Jessica loves running, being outdoors, and experiencing new things! She wrote "Finding Caroline" when she was still in high school, and it was published in *Teen Ink* magazine.

Kristen Noel Maxwell dedicates her poem, "Strength for the Bullied," to her boyfriend, Stephen, her best friend, Olivia, and her mother. She says that she wrote it for everyone who has ever gone through a difficult time and needed a hand to hold. Kristen can speak American Sign Language, and she loves to dance, sing, sew, write, and spin rifles! She plans to enlist in the United States Navy.

Audrey Miller likes to write poems and songs, take photographs, and work with computers. She wrote "My Facebook Bully" in hopes that it would help other teens who may have been bullied or who are still experiencing it. It is dedicated to someone special, who gave her the strength and courage to stand up for herself and for others.

Sharon Miller graduated high school in 2012. About "Think Before You Post," she says, "It's important to me that people realize how easy it is to forget the way gossip and bullying through social networking affects others. The human element that usually accompanies bullying is removed, but the power of an attack is still there. It's so easy for any of us to forget how easily we can hurt others via the Internet. Let's all amend our behavior and make everyone more comfortable!"

Jordan Molineux is part of a military family who has visited and lived in many places around the world, including Japan and England. She loves writing, acting, singing, and illustration, and also enjoys comics, story analysis, and puns. Jordan dedicates "Unfriendly Fire" to everyone who has suffered from bullying. She contributed to this collection because, she says, "My own middle-school experience could have been so much happier if I took control of the situation, represented myself fully, and beat bullies with kindness. I want others to realize their strength and unique presence shouldn't be compromised."

Michelle Moy took her photograph during the last week of a summer pre-college program in Boston. "We felt relieved it was over, but also stressed about the next coming school year," she says.

Alicia Murphy is studying psychology and art, and hopes to someday combine the two as an art therapist. Her photograph was the only single exposure among a whole roll of 35mm double exposures, and she was surprised and pleased by its unexpected clarity. She thanks Derick, the subject of the picture.

Sitav Nabi has loved writing from a young age and is currently an op-ed columnist for her local newspaper. Although she enjoys all subjects in school, Sitav has a special interest in science and mathematics. She also volunteers and tutors. "Dear Peers" was her first published piece at the age of 13 and consists of an accumulation of everything her bullies and supporters taught her. Sitav offers a special thank-you to her friends, family, teachers, and especially to her best friend, Miss Mary Louise Helwig-Rodriguez.

Amy Norton likes to provide opportunities for others to relax when she's not dealing with the "wonderful craziness" of her family. In high school, she cofounded a Christian coffeehouse with three friends, and she has also helped to create and organize a de-stressing college event called Keep Calm and Be a Kid. Amy wants people to understand that bullying may not be as black and white an issue as it sometimes seems, and she hopes that her story, "Confessions of an Ex-Bully," encourages kids to think about their actions. She thanks her family and dear friends in the 407.

Addison Nozell is the fifth child and first daughter in a family with six children. She competes on swim team and soccer and is a member of the FIRST robotics team at her high school. Addison also likes to be involved in various national and state political campaigns. She has a flock of backyard chickens, one of which (with some help from Addison's family) once painted a picture that was auctioned off to help to rebuild a playground. Addison wrote her poem, "What I Know," to support her sister, who was having a tough time at school with bullies.

Brandi O'Donnell recently graduated from high school. She works as a junior volunteer firefighter and likes to ski, read, and write; one day, she hopes to write a book. Brandi says, "People in the LGBTQ community should know they are never alone." She dedicates her piece, "Done Being a Victim," to Daina Elaine.

Michael Ortiz graduated high school this year and will be attending college. He loves listening to music and thanks his parents. He wrote "A Bully's Confession," and says, "Acceptance is key; to write this meant to accept all my flaws, which is the last stop to discovering myself."

Altay Sedat Otun is currently a college student. He is an avid traveler who has visited—among other places—North Korea, Turkey, China, Singapore, Thailand, and Cyprus. He loves experiencing new and different cultures and hopes to turn this passion into a successful career with the U.S. Department of State. Altay would like others to know that it's vital to understand that bullying is not always visible; the nonobvious forms of bullying can be the most hurtful. He thanks his boyfriend, Brian Yeh, for encouraging him to write "Uncivil Discourse."

Cameron P. says that writing "Past Imperfect" has helped him come to terms with his old mistakes by confessing them for others to read. He dedicates his piece to anyone he's knowingly put down in his lifetime, along with anybody who may have tried to correct him along the way. Cameron says, "Being a member of my high school's marching band and wind ensemble completely shaped my life throughout high school. Such a welcoming and nurturing group of people definitely opened my eyes to what a better person I could be."

Jessica Padilla says, "During my junior year, I was given a project to write an extensive research paper on cyberbullying. The assignment was called the 'Junior Humanity Project.' This inspired me to create a piece centered on bullying and donate it to my high school to be displayed in the hall." She thanks Kovida Putman, Kathy Skelton, Justin C. May, and "Stuffy."

Grace Park dedicates "I Forgive You" to everyone who's left a mark on her life, and she thanks God for blessing her with incredible friends and family. She would like to have met Fermat and asked him whether he really had a proof to his last theorem, and she wants to create a piece of art that people will look at and think about longer than it took for her to create.

Kaitlyn "Hope" Partin has always loved teaching and wants to major in early childhood education in college. She volunteers at her church's children's ministry and is involved in the youth group as well. Kaitlyn wrote "Cheyenne" in an attempt to capture a picture of what middle school was like. She dedicates it to her first-grade teacher, Mrs. Amy Cobb, for inspiring her to write, and to her mom for giving her unlimited hours to write.

Erika Pell is an aspiring writer who plans to double major in business administration and public relations/communications. As a ten-year 4-H member, she also shows market lambs, and she currently works as a server at IHOP. Erika thanks her parents. She says, "High school has never been easy, and I've never been the girl with lots of friends. Bullying of all kinds hurts; writing is my way of letting it out." Erika wrote about cyberbullying in "When 'Liking' is Hateful."

Ellena Pfeffer plans to be a professional photographer, working in fashion and portraits, because she loves face studies and photographing people in the moment. She would like to thank Erika H. for being a lovely model.

Emma Platoff has played the flute for ten years and loves many styles of music, from Shostakovich to Snoop Dogg. She is also on the staff of her school newspaper, works as an SAT tutor, and organizes charity performances in her hometown. About "Getting to the Root," Emma thinks that it's important to remember there's always more than one side to a story and more than one opinion to be heard, if one cares to listen.

Bridgette Rainey enjoys participating in varsity softball and basketball, and although she is still a high school student, has committed to playing softball for a large university when she graduates. When not playing sports, Bridgette participates in the integrity team and sources of strength clubs. Her piece, "Turn Around," can be found in the third chapter.

Andrew Ramos is president of two clubs, the California Scholarship Federation and the creative writing club, and vice president of another four. He has won awards for his photography and is currently the photo editor of his high school's newspaper. Andrew has also been part of a lacrosse team and done volunteer work. He thanks his AP English Language teacher and his best friends Tram-Le Harkins, Anna Richards, Emma Glassman Hughes, and Danielle Damper, for encouraging him to submit "Gayboy."

Lena Rawley is editor-in-chief of her school newspaper and publisher of her school's literary magazine. She played field hockey for four years and was captain of the state champion varsity squad. With "Attack of the Mean Girls," Lena wanted to share her experience with the world, letting the victims of bullying know they're not alone and they don't have to let this experience ruin their lives. She would like to thank her parents, and she dedicates her piece to anyone who's ever been bullied.

Natalie Rivera enjoys writing, swimming, and singing and was on the mock trial team and the drama club at her school. She has participated in student government for three years. Natalie's inspiration for "Some Say Good, I Say Pain" comes from a time when she noticed her bullies were being bullied. She reminded herself that she hated being bullied and knew they did too, so she decided to stand up and speak up for them, because no one had ever done that for her. She thanks her parents, her best friend, Naomi, and God.

Jessica C. Rockeman is currently a college student and having the time of her life with new experiences and new friends, although she does miss her mom and her cats sometimes. She is majoring in literature and creative writing, and she works two part-time jobs on campus (one in the campus women's center). She recently won first prize in a college writing contest! Jessica believes it is important for young girls to stick up for themselves and not to be afraid to use their voices. About her piece, "Take a Joke, Sweetheart," she thanks her mother for supporting both her writing and her feminism.

Nicole Rossi says she belongs to a big, eccentric family that has taught her tolerance and resilience and shown her pride in hard work and good manners. She enjoys being outside, drawing, working out, spending time with family, good books, movies, music, and baseball. Nicole recently graduated high school, where she wrote her poem, "Vultures."

James Sares graduated Harvard College in 2012 with a degree in social anthropology. In the future, he hopes to continue his education in philosophy and eventually become a professor, focusing on queer theory. "Silent No More" was originally his college essay, which he later edited and submitted to this anthology in solidarity with bullied LGBT youth across the country. James thanks Shirley Wood for providing a safe space for LGBT youth in an otherwise unfriendly environment.

Lily Seibert lives in New York with her parents, older brother, and dog. She loves running, playing basketball and softball, and singing. Lily is a sailor—during the past few summers, she's participated in sailing competitions along the East Coast. She is also a diehard New York Yankees fan and enjoys traveling. Lily's piece, "My Friends Were Bullies," was inspired by bullying she witnessed during fifth grade, and she wanted to highlight the important role of the bystander, because she believes that even those who seem to be uninvolved can always do something. She wants to thank G. Mo for being a great friend.

Libby Sellers has had the privilege of growing up in various countries, including the U.S., England, and Austria. She appreciates the breathtakingly beautiful places she's traveled and enjoys learning about other cultures. Libby played rugby in high school and also witnessed many instances of bullying. She dedicates her piece, "Four Chairs Down," to her brother, of whom she is very proud.

Chloe Sheppard loves photography, her dogs, family, and fashion. She says, "Thank you, Koumba, for letting me take a picture of your eye."

Sarah Shi joined her high-school newspaper editorial team freshman year and has since become the news editor. She has taken it as her job to share others' life stories with the world. In the future, Sarah would love to meet new people and to travel, particularly to Europe. She wrote "In Defense of the Golden Rule" after having a friend pass away from peer pressure and bullying. Sarah wants bullies to know that they may be able to hide behind their computer screens, but the damaging impact they have on others is open for all to see. She dedicates her piece to anyone who has been affected by bullying.

Shaughnelene Smith has recently been focusing on taking multiple photos of eyes. The model in her piece is her school roommate; Shaughnelene liked her dark complexion and how her skin complemented her scarf. She dedicates the piece to her dad.

Grace Elizabeth Stathos says, "I've been bullied for many years, and it hurts. It's time I take a stand. It's time we all take a stand. Thank you to everyone who has bullied me over the years. You changed me so much, but you made me who I am today, and I love who that is."

Carrie Sun created her artwork by layering plastic wrap on a scanner and pressing her face against it; it took many tries to get the right "smashed" look. She hopes that her piece conveys a sense of universality with regard to feelings of despair and depression, helping others believe they are not alone. She thanks her family.

Maria Sweeney is an illustration major who only recently began to seriously pursue an education in art. In her piece, she mixed her love of photography with another love: digital painting. Maria thanks Teen Ink for providing artists with an encouraging environment.

Shreekari Tadepalli began learning Indian classical dance at 4 and has continued to perfect its fundamentals even after her three-hour solo debut in 2010. She often finds herself sharing Eastern traditions in a Western environment, and she explains the meaning behind her movements to non-Indian audiences as a way to enhance their understanding of her cultural context. She wants to make sure that her story, "Love Thy Neighbor, Except for Some," is heard along with the countless others, all of which come from unique perspectives. She dedicates her piece to her parents.

Milan Thakkar is Chindian, with a Chinese mom and an Indian dad, but he's made his own choices and spent over a year in Costa Rica. There he graduated high school in 2012, and met his first real girlfriend. About "Singing His Praise," he writes, "There are always two sides to everything," and thanks his friend Patrick for opening his eyes.

Abby Weeden loves to take photos; she enjoys every part of the process and the stories they can tell. She says, "Thanks to my model and best friend, Bailey Rose, for always putting up with my elaborate and crazy ideas."

J. H. Yue produced her piece as part of a larger series of paintings based on "reverse ekphrasis": dramatic reinterpretations of poetry that inspired her. Allen Ginsberg's "Last Night in Calcutta" inspired this painting in particular. She thanks her parents and her eleventh-grade art teacher, Noor Ashour.

Hillel Zand is a native of New York City and will always be a diehard Yankees and Nets fan, but he is also a Canadian citizen. In his spare time he likes to play lacrosse and basketball, travel, watch movies, and hang out with friends. He also works with a philanthropic Jewish foundation. Hillel chose to write "Pride and Prejudice" to show that being part of a religion that makes up only 0.2 percent of the world's population is not always easy. He would like to thank his parents for helping nurture his Jewish and secular identities.

Permissions

ARTISTS

Index

WITHDRAWN

DEC — 2014